D1566486

EMOTIONAL INTELLIGENCE COACHING

Improving performance for leaders, coaches and the individual

Stephen Neale
Lisa Spencer-Arnell
Liz Wilson

KOGAN
PAGE

London and Philadelphia

Publisher's note

Every possible effort has been made to ensure that the information contained in this book is accurate at the time of going to press, and the publishers and authors cannot accept responsibility for any errors or omissions, however caused. No responsibility for loss or damage occasioned to any person acting, or refraining from action, as a result of the material in this publication can be accepted by the editor, the publisher or any of the authors.

First published in Great Britain and the United States in 2009 by Kogan Page Limited

120 Pentonville Road
London N1 9JN
United Kingdom
www.koganpage.com

525 South 4th Street, #241
Philadelphia PA 19147
USA

© Stephen Neale, Lisa Spencer-Arnell and Liz Wilson, 2009

ISBN 978 0 7494 5458 6

British Library Cataloguing-in-Publication Data

A CIP record for this book is available from the British Library.

Library of Congress Cataloging-in-Publication Data

Neale, Stephen.
    Emotional intelligence coaching : improving performance for leaders, coaches, and the individual / Stephen Neale, Lisa Spencer-Arnell, and Liz Wilson.
        p. cm.
    Includes index.
    ISBN 978-0-7494-5458-6
    1. Employees—Coaching of. 2. Emotional intelligence. 3. Performance—Psychological aspects. I. Spencer-Arnell, Lisa. II. Wilson, Liz. III. Title.
        HF5549.5.C53N43 2008
        658.3'124—dc22

2008031244

Typeset by JS Typesetting Ltd, Porthcawl, Mid Glamorgan
Printed and bound in India by Replika Press Pvt Ltd

Contents

Foreword

Sir John Whitmore,
Performance Consultants International

I believe that Emotional Intelligence and coaching are inseparable – in fact that emotionally intelligent people tend to behave in a coaching way even if they have not attended a coaching course. The authors of this book, I am delighted to see, reaffirm this connection throughout the book in a very clear and comprehensive way. It leaves the reader in no doubt about it, and will convince any aspiring coach that they need to attend to their own 'inner' work if they are to become an effective coach. The book focuses on Emotional Intelligence first, indicating that it is the foundation stone of good coaching; it goes on to address the basics of coaching and then to tie the two together.

The authors illustrate the points they are making very clearly with numerous examples, short stories and illustrative questions to help aspiring coaches to develop their understanding or existing coaches to refine their approaches. I was especially pleased to read the comprehensive sections later in the book addressing ethics and values. The pressures of the modern workplace in both the private and the public sectors at times invite shortcuts in standards to meet short-term goals. Coaches can play a significant role in advocating and exemplifying high standards, so much so that I regard this as a key function of the coaching profession. This book makes the case for this well.

Finally, as the profession of coaching grows so quickly these days, it behoves us to ensure that the training of coaches is done well. Professional ethics, standards and accreditation tests are being established, but some forms of coaching still diverge from the fundamentals on which coaching is based. This book will contribute much to keeping coaching on track and indeed raising the standards. In this book the references to the principles first advocated by Tim Gallwey in his ground-breaking book, *The Inner Game of Tennis*, and to the key coaching objective of building awareness and responsibility in oneself and others, are very important reminders to all coaches.

Foreword

Dr Patrick Williams,
Institute for Life Coach Training

At the heart of a human being are emotions, feelings, and the behavioural manifestations that come from those inner stirrings. What if people had the awareness to understand that every moment is one of choice, much of which is unconscious and habitual? Coaching assists clients to understand that as aware human beings we can choose to *respond* rather than *react* to situations in our life and work. If we can become more emotionally intelligent, we become capable of an expanded consciousness that leads to what Sir John Whitmore and other prominent coaches state as the ultimate goal of coaching: personal responsibility.

The concept of emotional intelligence became popular after the immense success of Daniel Goleman's books in the 1990s, *Emotional Intelligence: Why It Can Matter More Than IQ,* and *Working with Emotional Intelligence.* The business community was rocked by the research that overwhelmingly showed that up to 90 per cent of one's performance effectiveness was due to emotional savvy rather than technological knowledge.

The evidence is now clear that people skills are far more important than IQ when it comes to the bottom line. Not only are emotions very much a part of the work experience, but to a large degree they set the course that a company follows. The evidence behind the study of emotional intelligence gave way to language that encouraged the ability to talk about feelings, and their effect on workplace relationships. These so-called *soft skills* are now seen by today's corporate leaders as essential to a productive and resilient workplace... and this affects the company's profits as well.

Unlike IQ, which is unchanging from childhood on, emotional intelligence can be developed. In fact, it usually does become greater with age and maturity. The importance of developing one's emotional intelligence is essential to success in the workplace. Utilizing the power and energy of one's emotions leads to high motivation, and improves problem-solving and decision-making.

Coaches too need to be aware of, and developing in, the arena of EI. Coaching is an inter-developmental process, so the coach is more effective and more aware if they also improve their own emotional intelligence. People work better when feeling good, and feeling good about oneself and others requires good management of emotions. Some people are better at this than others, but everyone can learn.

Understanding emotions contributes toward building an emotionally intelligent organization. An emotionally intelligent organization can be imagined where:

- everyone communicates with understanding and respect;
- people set group goals and help others work toward them;
- enthusiasm and confidence in the organization are widespread.

The 'coach approach', coupled with emotional intelligence assessments, is a powerful combination in today's fast-moving and competitive marketplace. Investing in and improving *human capital* may be the missing link in long-term improvement in a company's working economic capital.

Stephen Neale, Lisa Spencer-Arnell and Liz Wilson have compiled in this volume the missing link between the promise of emotional intelligence and the practical application of the learning. That missing link is the coach approach. Coaching is what creates sustainability of change over time. And with increased emotional intelligence, a person could even learn to self-coach effectively.

Acknowledgements

We'd like to take this opportunity to thank a number of people who have contributed to this book coming together. We would like to say a big thank you to our colleague Andy for his support, great sense of humour and input on bringing this book together. We want to mention the people who generously gave their time and shared their wisdom and experience in the interviews they gave us; these include Sir John Whitmore – a leading light in the world of coaching, who is passionate about the difference coaching can make; Dr Patrick Williams, whose passion and knowledge make a great combination and contribution to coaching – we want to mention here the significant work Pat is doing to bring coaching to areas of the world where it wouldn't have reached otherwise. Thanks to Tim Gallwey – author of the fantastic 'Inner Game' series and Kirsten Poulsen, President of the European Mentoring and Coaching Council (EMCC), Denmark – passionate about improving the standards of our growing profession. Thank you to Morten Christensen of Statoil in Lithuania, Saulius Sabunas of AstraZeneca, Audrey Oliphant of Bank of Scotland, Ged Palmer of Gasco and Carla Ginn of Skandia who also gave us permission to share their experiences of coaching in organizations.

Thanks to Tim Sparrow and Amanda Knight for their hard work in searching for the truth about emotional intelligence. Thanks to Tim Sparrow and Jo Maddocks for providing a tool to fix the garden.

Finally, thanks to all the people we've worked with, learnt from and trained over the years.

Our personal acknowledgements

Steve – thank you always to my wife Sandra for her patience, understanding, humour, endless supply of healthy smoothies and love. Thanks to Oszkar for his endless supply of positive unconditional strokes, positive energy and fun.

Thank you to my parents for their unconditional support and love.

Thanks to the thousands of people I have worked with over the last few years for your energy and feedback on how you have used EI and coaching to change your lives.

Thanks to Keld Jensen for your inspiration, belief in me and my skills and opportunities.

Lisa – I'd like to thank three very important people in my life: my husband Gary for his understanding, love and great sense of fun; my beautiful daughter Grace for her energy, her spirit, her laughter and playfulness; and my Mum for her endless love and support, for her cooking and generosity of spirit.

I'd also like to thank my Dad, who's no longer with us, but he was a huge inspiration to me and a big believer in the potential we all have. Thanks to my special friends and family for your encouragement and love – you know who you are and thank you for being in my life.

Liz – thanks to my wonderful children Rachel and Simon for their love, enthusiasm and total enjoyment of life. Thank you to my parents Margaret and Granville for their eternal unconditional love and belief in me. Thanks to my amazing friends who encourage and support me, especially my sister Helen who has been a total inspiration this year. You all make my world a better place.

CONTACT THE AUTHORS

Steve Neale, Liz Wilson and Lisa Spencer-Arnell are Directors of the internationally renowned company, EI-Coach Training International Ltd (EICT). If you require information on any of the services we offer below, e-mail us at info@ei-coachtraining.com.

We hope you enjoy the book and as a thank you for reading it, we'd like to offer you the opportunity to receive our free ei-coach newsletter. It's packed with development ideas for leaders and coaches, the latest research from the world of EI and coaching, and personal development tips to improve your EI and coaching skills. To subscribe to this valuable source of wisdom, log on to http://www.ei-coachtraining.com and register online today. When you sign up, you will receive a free electronic toolkit for developing your EI.

Introduction

> *When dealing with people, remember that you are not dealing with creatures of logic, but creatures of emotion.*
>
> Dale Carnegie

About this book

This book is about what you can achieve when you combine the powerful ingredients of coaching and emotional intelligence (EI). It's a fresh approach to what can sometimes become a mechanical process and by that we mean people adopting just logical thinking and process to coaching. A large amount of energy goes into hiding emotion, especially in the workplace, and yet this provides the real powerful essence of who we are and what we achieve in life. We each have three brains (more on this later) and when you combine the three brains of the coach and the three brains of the coachee, magical things can happen – a definite case of 3 + 3 = 10!

While the book touches on the skills and knowledge that you need to be a great coach, it importantly explores in detail the attitudes and habits that are the elements which really impact performance. Never before have emotional intelligence and coaching been brought together in this way to help you develop your own and/or other people's performance.

Who is this book is for?

Whether you are an HR manager or director, a company leader or manager, a coach, trainer or consultant, or interested in people development and people being the best they can be, then this book is for you.

Why read this book?

If you are interested in people and particularly their development, then this book could be a significant resource for you, not to mention the organization you work in. There's a coaching toolkit, and a whole chapter on developing your emotional intelligence, which alone are worth their weight in gold.

How to get the most out of the book

We've written this book so you can read it from cover to cover or you can dip into the individual chapters and read them as stand alone sections. In each chapter we've intertwined inspirational quotes, case studies, interviews, activities and research, so whatever your preferred reading style is, you'll gain something out of it.

About the authors

Stephen Neale is Managing Director of EICT Ltd, an EI and coach training organization. He's a coach and trained psychologist, with degrees in both physiology and psychology, a professional certificate in psychodynamic counselling and a diploma in coaching. In recent years Stephen has specialized in EI and how it benefits leadership, teamwork and coaching. Stephen has presented, organized and taught courses in EI and coaching for a wide range of international organizations. A lot of his work has been centred in the Scandinavia and Baltic regions.

Lisa Spencer-Arnell is a Director of EICT and is a coach, mentor, trainer and qualified EI practitioner who has worked with many organizations in the UK and internationally. She has an MBA and a diploma in coaching and is passionate about standards and excellence. She is a member of The Chartered Institute of Personnel and Development (CIPD) and the International Coach Federation (ICF). Lisa has been involved in delivering coach training for several years and to date has trained more than 1,000 people in coaching skills in the UK, the United States and the Middle East.

Liz Wilson is a Director of EICT and is a coach, mentor, coach-supervisor and qualified EI practitioner. Liz has a BA (Hons) in Music and German, and holds a diploma in coaching, and certificates in mentoring and supervision. She coaches extensively on a one-to-one basis with a range of clients, from teenagers to MDs of large organizations, and she delivers courses in coaching, mentoring and supervision skills. Liz is a member of EMCC, Association for Coaching and CIPD and is passionate about standards and continued development.

To find out more about the authors, visit www.ei-coachtraining.com.

Note

The individual and team effectiveness tools referred to in this book were developed by Jo Maddocks of JCA Occupational Psychologists and Tim Sparrow, Measures for Success Limited.

ie and the ie logo *ie*, and te and the te logo *te* are trademarks of JCA (Occupational Psychologists) Limited. JCA reserves all rights and is the exclusive worldwide publisher.

THE HAPPY GARDENER

Charlie was an unhappy gardener. His whole life had been dedicated to growing the perfect garden, but each year he found he got the same, dismal results: the flowers died, the grass lost its colour, the weeds took over and the local wildlife stayed away.

Depressed by another poor year of lacklustre results, Charlie decided to take a walk by his favourite river. Normally, this was a quiet place he could go and dwell on his failures, but on this occasion his thoughts were disturbed by a wise man sitting by the river edge. Unaccustomed to seeing anyone on this quiet path, Charlie decided to say hello. The wise man slowly turned his head and what he said surprised Charlie: 'It seems that you are unhappy my friend. Your eyes look sad, your posture is stooping, I see sadness in your face and your energy feels low.' At first Charlie was surprised; a simple 'Hello' was all he was expecting. He was also stunned by the accuracy of the wise man's observations and found himself agreeing with everything he had heard.

'How could you know that?' he replied, 'You don't even know me.'

'You don't have to know someone to pick up on their emotions,' the wise man replied. 'Would you like to sit and talk? I would love to listen to what is on your mind.'

Charlie did not normally find it easy to talk to others, particularly complete strangers. But this time something was different. The sense of calmness, trust and positive energy he felt being around this man moved him towards his quick response 'Sure, why not.'

'What's on your mind?' asked the wise man. Charlie hesitated and thought carefully about his response. He decided to be honest: 'I am pretty unhappy actually. All my life I've wanted to be a successful gardener and all my life I have failed.'

'Would you like to change that?' inquired the wise man.

'Absolutely. I can't think of anything that would make me happier,' responded Charlie.

Sensing the commitment in Charlie's voice and body, the wise man then told Charlie that he could help him. 'All the solutions to your problem are already inside you. If you are willing to change, then I will help you think, feel and behave like a successful gardener.'

'Fabulous. How long will it take? Can I get what I need today?'

'Patience, belief and commitment are what you need to succeed my friend, and the rest will follow with time. Today I can help you to raise awareness of the things you must change, but true, lasting change will take longer. If you only show commitment today, then you will resort to your old habits and nothing will change. If you will work with me for the next few months, then I promise you will have the garden of your dreams by next summer. I can also promise you the changes you make during those months will last for the rest of your life. How does that sound?'

'That sounds great. What are a few months if you get to change for the rest of your life?'

The wise man added, 'Before we start I must tell you one more thing. What you will learn during this journey is very powerful. You'll learn how to use your own strengths to make the most of the tools at your disposal in your garden. You'll learn to work with the garden and the changing seasons to make it beautiful. You'll learn how you have to be to adapt when something doesn't grow or look how you want it to look. You'll learn how to bounce back from your disappointments and find different ways to get what you want.'

'You can help me do all that?'

'Yes, I can. Now, tell me what you believe about your skills as a gardener. What thoughts enter your mind when you think of you gardening?'

'If I'm absolutely honest, I've kind of given up hope. I don't believe I've got what it takes and seriously doubt if I can ever create the garden I have dreamed of for so long.'

'And how do these thoughts affect the way you garden?'

Charlie paused. He had never considered there may be a connection between his thoughts and his actions before. After some thought he replied, 'Now I think about it, I guess I haven't been making much of an effort lately. I have been spending less and less time in the garden and haven't bothered replacing my broken garden tools. I guess I didn't see the point.'

Throughout the next few months, the wise man met with Charlie once each month at the same spot by the river. At each meeting, the wise man listened and asked Charlie some thought-provoking, sometimes challenging questions. After each meeting, Charlie went away with various things to do, sometimes just to challenge the way he thought, but more often than not to actually do things differently.

Charlie began to notice that he was more willing to try different things on his own, feeling more confident that he had good ideas, knew more than he realized about gardening, and that it felt really good. He started to believe he *was* a good gardener after all.

After several months Charlie had done what he never thought he could do. The weeds had all gone, replaced by a beautiful array of flowers and plants. The grass was greener than ever before and the local wildlife filled the garden with energy and life. Enjoying spending his time in these beautiful surroundings he had created, Charlie started thinking about how the wise man had helped him since they first met. The interesting thing was that the more he reflected on it, the more he realized that the man had given him little or no advice along the way. In fact, the only advice he could remember was that sitting down and reflecting on what he had done each day was a great habit to develop. And Charlie vowed to himself there and then that he would always do this, not only when things were fine and vibrant in his garden, but also when it needed more attention because the weeds had begun to surface again.

Figure 0.1 The happy gardener

1

What is emotional intelligence?

> *Destiny is not a matter of chance, it is a matter of choice. It is not a thing to be waited for, it is a thing to be achieved.*
>
> William Jennings Bryan

IT'S ALL ABOUT PERFORMANCE

Let's get one thing straight from the start – developing your emotional intelligence (EI) will improve your performance. EI is not about lots of unclear, touchy-feely ideas that are fun to read about or experience in a training programme, but when you go back to work, nothing really happens. Developing your EI will take time, but will lead to sustainable behaviour changes that will improve the way you manage yourself and the way you work with others.

Just some of the advantages of developing your emotional intelligence are:

- improved relationships;
- improved communication with others;
- better empathy skills;
- acting with integrity;
- respect from others;
- improved career prospects;
- managing change more confidently;
- fewer power games at work;
- feeling confident and positive;
- reduced stress levels;

▓   increased creativity;
▓   learning from mistakes.

This book will substantiate the above claims with both theoretical and practical evidence that EI and performance are connected. Rather than being just another fad, EI is here to stay. Through skilled facilitation and coaching, EI development for individuals, teams and whole organizations will lead to a more productive, successful and sustainable business culture. By combining relevant theory, scientific evidence, case studies and practical activities, this book will help you to understand and apply the powerful combination of emotional intelligence and coaching.

There has been a massive growth in the popularity of EI since Daniel Goleman's publication, *Emotional Intelligence: Why it can matter more than IQ* (1996). Increasingly, people have recognized the important role emotions play in our actions. When you replace the word 'action' with 'performance', you can start to understand the impact EI can have on a company's bottom line.

In his series of 'Inner Game' books, Timothy Gallwey explains performance in a simple equation:

$P = p - i$
(Performance = potential - interferences)

What Gallwey is saying is that each of us has the potential to improve our performance, but what stops us are individual interferences. In EI terms, the interferences we all possess are essentially negative attitudes, beliefs and habits that prevent us from performing as well as we could.

Activity: Your interferences

Take a moment to think about and make a list of your negative attitudes (interferences) in relation to various work tasks. For example, do you have any negative attitudes connected to the following?

▓   Giving a presentation.
▓   Attending a team meeting.
▓   Writing a report.
▓   Your annual performance review.
▓   The new IT system your company has introduced.
▓   The 'difficult' colleague you have to work with.
▓   Your boss.

How could these attitudes be impacting on your behaviour? How would your performance improve if you had the opposite, positive attitude? (For example, 'Team meetings are boring and a waste of time' could become, 'Team meetings are interesting and productive').

WHAT IS EMOTIONAL INTELLIGENCE?

Emotions are involved in everything we do: every action, decision and judgement. Emotionally intelligent people recognize this and use their thinking to manage their emotions rather than being managed by them.

Just like the term 'coaching', which will be addressed in Chapter 2, different theorists define EI in different ways. We agree with the definition offered by Sparrow and Knight in *Applied EI* (2006):

Emotional intelligence is the habitual practice of:

- using emotional information from ourselves and other people;
- integrating this with our thinking;
- using these to inform our decision making to help us get what we want from the immediate situation and from life in general.

Put another way: EI is using thinking about feeling (and feeling about thinking) to guide our behaviour.

This will lead to better management of ourselves and better relationships with others.

HOW MANY BRAINS HAVE YOU GOT?

To understand how we define EI, it is first important to understand some things about how our brains work. The evolved human brain can be split into three different parts, as illustrated by Paul MacLean's triune brain model (1973); see Figure 1.1.

Many millions of years ago we crawled out of the water in the form of reptiles. At that time we possessed only the most primitive part of our modern brain, which is the brainstem surrounding the top of the spinal cord. This *reptile brain* regulates basic life functions such as breathing, as well as controlling reflex reactions and movements. Rather than thinking or learning, this primitive brain keeps basic functions in the body running smoothly, such as telling us when we are hungry or need sleep. It therefore plays an essential part in our survival.

As we developed as a species, our brain grew outwards, forming what is now known as the limbic brain (also called the mammalian or *emotional brain*). This unconscious part of our brain is our emotional centre, housing our values, beliefs and attitudes and generating the emotions that they trigger.

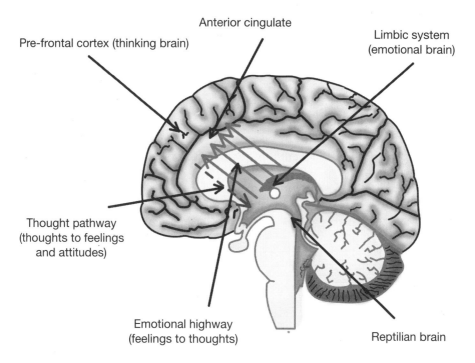

Anterior cingulate

Pre-frontal cortex (thinking brain)

Limbic system
(emotional brain)

Thought pathway
(thoughts to feelings
and attitudes)

Emotional highway
(feelings to thoughts)

Reptilian brain

Figure 1.1 The triune brain

In more recent times on the evolutionary timescale, we grew our third and final brain. Known as the neo-cortex, it contains the prefrontal cortex, which is responsible for thought (the *thinking brain*).

With the application of modern techniques of brain imaging, scientists have been able to start measuring activity in different parts of the brain at any one time. Perhaps not surprisingly, our unconscious, emotional brain is much more active than our logical, thinking brain. Estimates show that up to 6 billion nerve cells are firing in any one second in our emotional brain, compared to somewhere around the surprisingly small figure of 100 neuronal stimulations in our logical brain. What's more, as our brain grew outwards, it developed extensive neuronal connections leading from our emotional brain to our logical brain (and to the rest of our body). In other words, our emotional brain is sending messages to our logical brain and around the body every second. We have also developed neuronal connections from our thinking brain to our emotional brain, but as the brain grew outwards, these connections are much fewer in number.

A simple way to think of this is that the emotional brain is connected to the thinking brain via a large highway of nerve cells. The connections moving in the opposite direction, from thinking to feeling, are more like a small pathway. However, often our thinking brain does not become consciously aware of the emotion being sent from our emotional brain. Instead, this emotion is processed unconsciously by an area of the brain called the anterior cingulate, which leads to us behaving in the same habitual way that we usually do, paying little or no attention to the emotion we are feeling or the attitude it is connected to.

The lion and the tamer

By and large, New Year resolutions don't work. At the same time, people regularly fail to apply their 'will power' and resort to old habits. Given the relative roles and influence of the unconscious emotional brain and the conscious logical brain, this is not at all surprising. The thinking brain is like a lion tamer and the emotional brain is the lion. Through careful, patient and repeated efforts, the tamer can learn to tame the lion and manage the beast in an effective way. However, ultimately, the lion is always the more powerful animal, representing the thousands of automatic operations we carry out every second outside of conscious awareness. We must always remember that the lion has been around much longer than the tamer and is always capable of taking command of a situation. The tamer must always treat the lion with respect, working in harmony with it in order for things to operate smoothly and safely. The consequences of the tamer and the lion not being in harmony could be catastrophic.

We often think of rapport between ourselves and other people, but what about the rapport between your thinking brain and your emotional brain? If the two brains are fighting against each other, the emotional brain will win every time. This would explain why your attempts to give up smoking, lose weight through dieting, or take more exercise often fail. Your logical brain knows that not smoking, eating healthy food and exercise are good for you. However, your emotional brain governs a set of attitudes, emotions and habits that are not in harmony with this logic.

The good news is that it is possible for the tamer to train and manipulate the lion in certain ways, distracting it from harmful actions and focusing its attention on more positive ones. But never forget, the lion is always much more aware of what is going on within us and around us than the tamer. Your lion will communicate with you via feelings, intuitions, dreams and physical symptoms, and the more you listen to it and understand it, the more likely you are to create a successful tamer and lion relationship.

I feel, therefore I am

So, given that our emotional brain has a much greater 'fire power' than our thinking brain, our thinking brain is often subservient to and influenced by our emotional brain. It is therefore more accurate to replace the popular philosophical statement of 'I think, therefore I am' with 'I feel, therefore I am.'

This also raises big questions about our education, where we are measured and tested on logical, thinking-brain challenges and tasks. How about the world of business? Do you have any senior managers who have been promoted purely on their subject-specific knowledge? Have you found that many of these managers have problems managing the new demands that senior management places on them? How about their relationship management? Are they always good at leading, motivating, coaching, listening and empathizing with others? Just because an individual's thinking brain is capable of doing the task, it doesn't necessarily mean that their more influential emotional brain is also sufficiently developed.

A study carried out in 1976 by The Carnegie Institute of Technology supports this. In an investigation into the reasons why people are successful in business, the Institute concluded that up to 85 per cent of financial success is due to skills in human engineering, while only 15 per cent is due to technical knowledge. For example, if we take a job such as marketing manager, there are lots of people out there with the same level of marketing expertise, but only those few with highly developed human engineering skills will achieve sustainable, top-level success. Human engineering essentially comes from two of the key aspects of emotional intelligence, namely self-management and relationship management.

Further evidence supporting the 'emotions matter more than logic' idea comes from Daniel Kahneman's Nobel Prize winning claim of 2002. Basically, Kahneman stated that all human beings are irrational and that we would rather do business with someone we like and trust than someone we don't like and don't trust. This is even true if the person we like is offering a lower quality product at a higher price.

Think about yourself. Are all your business decisions based on logic? Did you buy that new laptop because you really needed it or because you liked the salesperson and you think having that laptop in meetings will make you feel good?

It's all about attitude!

First we make our attitudes. Then our attitudes make us.

Dennis Waitley

Everything we do involves the experiential triangle of thoughts, emotions and actions; see Figure 1.2. In other words, whatever the situation, we are always thinking, feeling and doing and these three things are always connected. This is completely consistent with how our brains work.

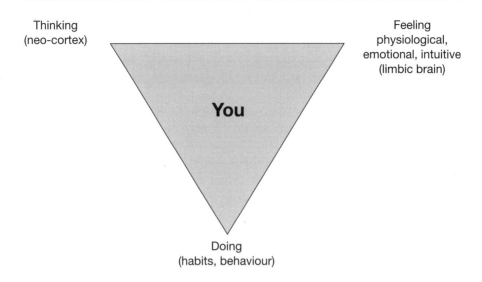

Figure 1.2 Thinking, feeling, doing triangle

During our childhood years, when our brains are developing at a rapid rate, we develop hundreds of attitudes about the world around us, mostly based on our experiences and what we are taught by peers and adults. Our attitudes play a vital part in how we react to things emotionally and how we then act. The following example, adapted from the stimulus response model developed by Griffin (Griffin and Tyrrell, 2001), demonstrates the role attitudes can play in the stimulus to response process.

Sally and the spider

Step 1 *(stimulus)*: Sally sees a large spider crawling across the floor towards her.

Step 2: This triggers unconscious attitudes in Sally's limbic brain: 'Spiders are bad and dangerous and I hate them.'

Step 3: This attitude is tagged to an emotion that Sally experiences: *fear.*

Step 4: Strong emotional signals are sent to Sally's logical brain (via her emotional motorway) and the rest of her body.

Step 5 *(response)*: Sally reacts by screaming and running away, repeating a habitual response she has carried out many times before (her anterior cingulate automatically and unconsciously processes this emotion before her logical brain has time to rationalize the situation).

Sally's actions stem from her attitude towards spiders and the emotion linked to this attitude (in this case, fear). This type of strong emotional reaction is what Daniel Goleman refers to as an 'emotional hijack'. Essentially, a hijack occurs when we allow our attitudes and the emotions they generate to take over our thinking and behaviour.

For someone who does not have negative attitudes towards spiders, the emotions generated and actions would be very different. For example, for someone who has pet spiders the attitude might be, 'I like spiders,' the emotion might be 'excitement' and the action might be to walk over and have a closer look at the spider.

Activity: Your emotional hijacks

Stop and think for a moment about any recent emotional hijacks you have experienced. For example, how did you react the last time:

- Another car driver pulled out in front of you causing you to brake?
- Your boss asked you to do something you really don't enjoy?
- You got caught in a really bad rain shower?
- Your computer crashed?
- You were confronted by something you are afraid of?
- Someone pushed in front of you in a queue?

Attitudes play a fundamental role in our levels of emotional intelligence. The following example demonstrates how attitudes are linked to performance.

Mike the scientist

Mike used to like drawing and painting as a young child. Both his parents and his school teachers discouraged this, advising him instead to focus on more logical, scientific subjects. ('You will never be good at art son, but focus on your maths and you will be successful.') As a result, Mike developed an unconscious attitude: 'I am not creative.' (This stems from a fundamental need to be liked by others, that we all have.)

Perhaps not surprisingly, Mike graduated in IT and became an IT department manager working for a pharmaceutical company. One day, his boss called him into the office and said he wanted Mike to try something new. The company needed to make some changes and he wanted Mike to go away for a week and be creative, coming up with some innovative approaches to how the IT department could operate. The mere mention of the word 'creative' triggered Mike's unconscious negative attitude about his creativity, which immediately triggered some negative emotions (fear, irritation and frustration). These emotions influenced Mike's thoughts about the task and as a result he found himself thinking things like, 'That's just not me, I can't do that' and, 'It's unfair to ask me to do that, it's not my role.' For a whole week these negative thoughts and feelings continued. The result? Mike failed to come up with any new approaches.

As we can see from this example, attitudes play a vital role in the thought-feeling-action triangle of events. Mike's childhood attitudes generated emotions and thoughts about creativity, thus impacting on performance.

What if Mike had positive attitudes towards creativity? What if his new default attitude was, 'I am a creative person and love generating new ideas'? When asked by his boss to create something new, this positive attitude would probably trigger positive emotions such as excitement and interest, which would lead to thoughts such as, 'Great, I can't wait to do this, when can I get started?' These positive thoughts and emotions mean there will be a much greater chance of Mike performing the task successfully (psychologists refer to this as the 'self-fulfilling prophecy'). As Henry Ford once stated: 'Whether you think you can, or think you can't… you're right.'

EMOTIONAL INTELLIGENCE – TWO ASPECTS

To be successful requires effective awareness, control and management of your own emotions, and awareness and understanding of other people. EI therefore embraces two aspects of intelligence: 1) understanding yourself, your goals, intentions, responses, behaviour and all; 2) understanding others and their feelings.

In his 1980's research into multiple intelligences, Howard Gardner describes these two aspects of intelligence as *intrapersonal intelligence* – being intelligent in picking up what is going on inside us and doing what we need to do about it; and *interpersonal intelligence* – being intelligent in picking up what is going on in other people and between other people and doing what we need to do about it. Figure 1.3 shows how these two types of intelligence are connected to emotional intelligence.

We will define what each of these different aspects of EI mean later in this chapter. Here is a case study demonstrating how a lack of self-management and relationship management can show itself in the workplace.

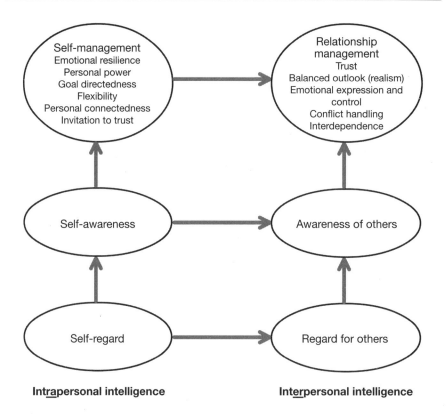

Figure 1.3 How intrapersonal and interpersonal intelligence are connected to emotional intelligence

(Adapted from Sparrow and Maddocks, 2000)

Barry and Mark

Barry was a successful sales manager working for a pharmaceutical company. His results over the last six months had been particularly impressive, so his boss decided to reward him. He called Barry into his office and told him he was so pleased with Barry's performance that the company would pay for a two-week Caribbean cruise for Barry and his family.

Naturally, Barry was very pleased and wanted to share his happiness with his colleagues. The first person he saw was Mark, a colleague also working as a sales manager in the same department. When he told Mark, he was surprised by Mark's reaction. Even though Mark said he was pleased for him, Barry got the impression that Mark was in some way disappointed. In actual fact, Mark took the news quite badly. He felt angry and started to ask himself why it wasn't him going on the cruise. Mark started telling other colleagues in the department about the unfair decision and how angry he was. He even started spreading rumours about Barry in an attempt to make him look bad and reinforce Mark's belief that this was unfair. He also took the negative emotions home with him, and told his wife what a terrible job he has and how his boss doesn't like him. In fact, Mark held on to these negative emotions and spent the next few weeks at work feeling sorry for himself, still unable to come to terms with the injustice he felt he had suffered.

What did Mark do wrong and how is this connected to attitudes and emotions? First of all, when Barry told him the good news he reacted badly. Why? Because Mark had the attitudes, 'My boss doesn't like me' and 'I'm not appreciated', he experienced negative emotions when he heard the news. He felt angry at the decision, jealous and sad. Emotional intelligence is about managing your emotions. Here's what Mark could have done to manage them and make his subsequent behaviour more effective:

Step 1:   Pause and ask himself what emotions he was feeling and why.
Step 2:   Take control of these emotions by using his thinking.
Step 3:   Improve his actions.

So here's how the story could have turned out if Mark had used his emotional intelligence.

On hearing the news of Barry's holiday, Mark wanted to feel happy for Barry, but instead found himself experiencing negative emotions. Mark went away and asked himself what emotions he felt and why. He felt *jealous* because he felt he deserved the holiday and was a dedicated loyal worker. He felt *angry* because he wanted to know what he had to do to get a holiday and felt he deserved the reward. He also felt *sad* because he really liked Barry and was going to miss the banter they had in the office while Barry was away. Mark decided to manage these emotions and take control of them. He went to see his manager and explained to him he would really like a holiday too and asked his manager what was needed to warrant this reward. He then moved his thoughts to the sadness and decided this would be a good opportunity to get to know some other colleagues. He called James, another sales manager, and asked if he would like to grab lunch later that week. Mark soon felt better about Barry's reward and found himself feeling quite positive about the situation.

So, the message is clear: *we need to use our thinking to manage our feelings before we take action.*

CAN YOU IMPROVE YOUR EMOTIONAL INTELLIGENCE?

Here's the good news – all attitudes can be changed if we want to change them, so all aspects of EI can be developed and improved. There are five basic principles that form the foundation of emotional intelligence:

1. EI is not one single thing, but is made up of a mixture of attitudes, feelings and thoughts and the actions that result from them.
2. EI predicts performance.
3. EI can be measured.
4. EI can be changed.
5. Developing your EI will impact on all areas of your life.

1. EI is not one single thing

Contrary to the implication of some popular models of EI, emotional intelligence cannot be simplified into one basic score. Unlike IQ, it is impossible to measure an individual's EI as a single number. EI is made up of a complex mixture of interrelated attitudes, feelings and habits.

2. EI predicts performance

As we described earlier, EI is directly linked to performance and this connection can be understood using Gallwey's $P = p - i$ equation.

3. EI can be measured

Through self-evaluation and 360-degree feedback emotional intelligence can be measured. As we said above, what is being measured is a mixture of attitudes and habits. Later in this chapter we will outline the 16 measurable scales of EI in more detail.

4. EI can be changed

Each of the above areas of emotional intelligence can be changed and developed. However, there is no quick fix for this, so attending a two-day training programme will not dramatically change your EI. Evidence shows that it takes around 21 days to change an attitude.

For true, lasting development to take place, all change should be looked at using the four main elements of the KASH model described in *Applied EI* (Sparrow and Knight, 2006):

Knowledge
Attitudes
Skills
Habits

What did the last training course you attended focus on? In the majority of cases, the answer will be knowledge and skills. However, if your attitudes about yourself and the training aren't right, all the knowledge and skills training in the world won't make any significant difference. Take, for example, the employee who doesn't want to be on the training but has been told to attend. Or what about the person on the presentation skills training who has an attitude 'I hate standing in front of groups. It is just not me'?

Another way of looking at this is what we call the 'training iceberg'. Most training focuses entirely on knowledge and skills (using our thinking brain), but as Figure 1.4 shows, deeper changes at the attitude (emotional brain) and habit level also need to be addressed if sustainable change is going to occur.

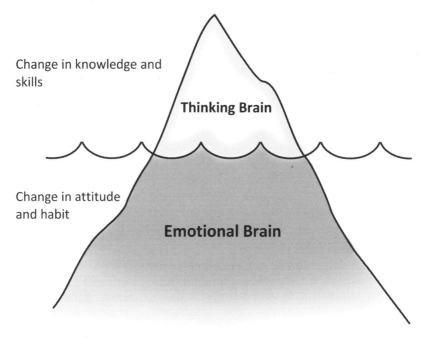

Figure 1.4 The training iceberg

For true lasting development to take place, attitudes and habits (behaviour) connected to those attitudes usually need to be developed. For example, if you want to develop your awareness of others, applying the KASH model might look like this:

Knowledge: Reading about awareness of others and understanding what it is and how you can develop it.

Attitudes: Understanding and challenging the negative attitudes you have connected to awareness of others (eg 'He doesn't listen to me, so why should I listen to him').

Skills: Practising using the knowledge you have learnt about actively listening to others, listening to what they say and the body language messages they send out.

Habits: Gradually changing the way you act when in conversation with others, paying more attention, interrupting people less and asking more open questions to help understand them better.

5. Developing your EI will impact on all areas of your life

Because EI is essentially about attitudes and feelings, it follows that if aspects of our EI change, then we change as people. It may be that your company wants you to develop your flexibility so you are more constructive about the department changes taking place. If you improve your attitudes towards flexibility, this will also impact on other areas of your life. You may, for example, find yourself wanting to do different things with your family, taking up a new sport, or trying out food that you wouldn't have eaten before.

So, if through skilled facilitation and coaching, you develop your EI, it is not just your job performance that will improve. You will also experience changes with your family and friends, at weekends, on holiday and in just about any situation you face.

MEASURING EI

There are a growing number of tools available to measure EI. In our opinion, by far the most advanced tools are the individual, team and organizational effectiveness tools developed by Tim Sparrow and Jo Maddocks. The individual effectiveness^{TM} tool measures your EI on 16 different, interrelated scales, which were outlined in Figure 1.3.

Here is a quick summary of what each scale means. Later we will look at how these scales are relevant to coaching (Chapter 3), can be used for self-development (Chapter 5) and can be used by a coach to help facilitate development in others (Chapter 9).

Regard

Self-regard (or self-esteem)

How much do you value yourself as a person? Self-regard is about who you are, not what you do. All too often people develop conditions of worth to substitute for self-regard, focusing on what they achieve or own rather than who they are. If we like and accept ourselves it will have a positive impact on all situations.

Regard for others

How much do you value others as people, as distinct from what they do? How often do you find yourself making judgements of others based on your own values? It is perfectly acceptable to criticize other people's behaviour (as long as it is constructive criticism), but never acceptable to judge them as a person. For example, 'What you did was stupid' is very different from thinking or saying, 'You are stupid.'

Awareness

Self-awareness

How much are you in touch with your intuition and feelings? How well do you listen to what your body is telling you? Hundreds of times a day our emotional brain communicates with us via feelings. People with low self-awareness often don't notice this or learn from it.

Activity

Press your pause button (stop and think) when you are feeling something and ask yourself:

- What emotion am I feeling right now?
- Where am I feeling it in my body? (Butterflies in my stomach? Tension in my neck?)
- Why am I feeling it?
- What triggered it?
- What attitudes, beliefs or values is it connected to?

Awareness of others

How well tuned in are you to the feeling states of others? How well do you pick up on other people's non-verbal cues telling you how they are feeling? Do you regularly show empathy towards others and really listen to what they are telling you?

Self-management

Emotional resilience

How well do you bounce back when things go wrong? It is a fact that we will all experience negative things in our lives that will trigger negative emotions. This could range from your train being cancelled to being fired from your job or losing a close friend. Emotional resilience is about how effectively you recover from these situations, turning negative attitudes, thoughts and emotions into more positive ones.

Personal power

How much do you take control of your life, seeing yourself as being responsible for your own actions? The opposite of personal power is to see yourself as a victim, always looking to blame other people or things for your failure to succeed.

Goal directedness

How clear are you on your goals and how much do your attitudes, beliefs and actions support you by moving you towards these goals? Or do you regularly find yourself procrastinating, looking for excuses or spending time on things that will not help you to achieve your goals?

Flexibility

Change is a fact of life. All of us will experience regular changes at work and at home. Flexibility is about how free you feel to adapt your thoughts, attitudes and behaviour in times of change, seeing change as an opportunity for creating something new and better rather than resisting change and always trying to hold on to the way things used to be.

Personal connectedness

How well do you make significant connections with others by being open and honest about your true feelings? How easy do you find it to be honest with yourself about how you feel and then be prepared to communicate this appropriately to others?

Invitation to trust

How much do you invite the trust of others by being consistent, true to your word and reliable? Or are you a person who regularly changes opinion just to be liked by those around you, or maybe you regularly fail to keep promises and say things you don't really mean?

Relationship management

Unlike all the previous scales above, which are linear (more is better), the relationship management scales are bipolar. In other words, it is not good to go to either extreme on any of these scales, but better to find a healthy balance in the middle.

Trust

It is not good to totally trust all people all of the time, as this may lead to disappointment and allow others to take advantage of you. At the same time, the world would be a very lonely and negative place if you are always suspicious and never trust anyone in any situation.

Emotionally intelligent trust lies somewhere in the middle, being carefully trusting of people, and remembering when it may be wise to keep things to yourself until that trust has been earned.

Balanced outlook

Do you have a tendency to be pessimistic, focusing on what's wrong with things and highlighting problems rather than solutions? ('It's too hot today', 'It's too cold for me', 'I don't like this flavour', 'We should have gone to Spain instead.')

Do you always assume everything will be fine without taking the necessary action to make sure it is? Do you set unrealistic goals that you regularly fail to achieve?

Having a balanced outlook is about generally keeping a positive attitude about things but also being realistic and objective about the likelihood of things succeeding and turning out the way you want.

Emotional expression and control

You will experience hundreds of different emotions every day. Emotions can change very quickly – one moment you may be feeling relaxed and happy, the next you might be angry because somebody drove into the back of your car.

Do you bottle up your emotions during the day, believing it is not appropriate or right to show how you are feeling? Do you have no control filter at all, always allowing your emotions to burst out into your behaviour, however inappropriate it may be?

Emotional expression and control is about choosing when to allow your emotions to show, feeling free to express your emotions, but also having enough control to select when and how you do this.

Conflict handling

Conflict is a fact of life. Every day you will experience conflicts, whether they are small things ('I want to share a bottle of red wine but my friend wants a bottle of white') or more important things ('I want to move to Spain but my husband wants to stay in the UK').

Do you regularly shy away from conflict, feeling uncomfortable and believing that all conflict is bad? Do you use humour or other avoidance techniques to prevent direct discussion about disagreements?

Do you view conflict as a battle, where there is a winner and a loser and you want to be the winner? Do you often find yourself shouting, interrupting and not listening to others, determined to have things your way?

Both of these extremes (passive and aggressive) are ineffective ways of managing conflict. A healthy balance between these two approaches is being assertive; standing up for your own wants and needs while at the same time being prepared to listen to, understand and compromise with others.

Interdependence

Do you depend too much on others, worried about how successful you would be on your own? Do you link your own identity too much with those around you, finding false security in the fact you have successful friends or are married to a great partner?

Do you believe that the only way to get something done properly is to do it yourself? Do you think working with others holds you back and that you are much better off doing things on your own?

Interdependence is about having healthy attitudes about working with others. While recognizing that you can be successful on your own, it is about truly believing that cooperating with others will lead to something more productive (having a 1+1 = 4 philosophy).

A note about reflective learning

While not an aspect of emotional intelligence itself, an essential quality needed to develop your emotional intelligence is reflective learning. This is the habit of looking back on experiences, and reflecting on how you and others thought, felt and behaved at the time. The following case study demonstrates how reflective learning can be useful.

Patricia and the overtime favour

Patricia always hated starting new jobs. Generally, in any situation where she was meeting new people, she felt uncomfortable and anxious because she wanted others to like her.

Just two weeks after starting as an administrative assistant in a new company, one of her colleagues asked her for a favour. Jill explained that her boss had asked her to do some overtime on Saturday because there was an essential mailshot that needed to be ready for Monday morning. Jill explained that the weekend was really bad for her and asked Patricia if she could take on the work instead. Patricia responded immediately by saying yes, even though she knew she had promised to take her kids away for the weekend. For the rest of the day, she regretted this and felt anxious about telling her kids. She was also annoyed with herself for putting others first. However, rather than letting these negative emotions take over, Patricia spent some time thinking about what happened. She realized first of all that she had said yes because she was keen to be liked by her colleague. At the time she was asked, she had an uncomfortable feeling in her stomach, which she linked to her need to be liked by others. She then asked herself if, had she said no, Jill would have liked her less. The clear answer was no – it would have been perfectly acceptable to explain that she had made other plans for the weekend. Patricia promised herself that she would stop and think before making an immediate reply when faced with a similar situation again.

The important think about reflective learning is not to judge yourself or others for feelings and attitudes you have right now. Instead, focus on behaviours you will change the next time a similar situation happens. So, in Patricia's case, it is fine for her to say to herself, 'Immediately saying yes was wrong, and next time I will stop and think before I give my answer.' However, if Patricia says to herself, 'I was stupid,' this is making a judgement of herself and will only damage her self-regard.

SUSTAINABLE CHANGE TAKES TIME

As EI development is about changing attitudes and the habits connected to these attitudes, it takes time. Human beings are creatures of habit, and we developed many of those habits during our childhood years. Sometimes habits are a good thing and prevent our logical brain from having to process the masses of information it could potentially have to deal with in a day. For example, think about cleaning your teeth when you are getting ready for work in the morning. This is an automatic task that most of us don't have to consciously think about to perform. Imagine being faced with your toothbrush and a tube of toothpaste every morning but having no idea what to do with them and having to try to work it out each day!

However, many of the habits we form are not helpful to us. These are the habits that developing your EI will help to change. For example, let's say you are in the habit of saying nothing in team meetings because you have the attitude, 'Everyone here is more knowledgeable than me so there's no point in giving my opinion.' While you maintain this attitude and the habit of silence connected to it, your team is missing out on a valuable extra opinion that could lead to improved team performance.

How do we change a habit?

When we are learning something new, we all have to go through four stages:

1. *Unconsciously incompetent.* You don't know how to do something and are unaware and unconcerned about it (eg, I can't drive a car and have never really thought about it).
2. *Consciously incompetent.* You begin to learn something new but realize it's more difficult that you thought. We often feel irritated at this stage because we can't do it (eg, you know how you are supposed to drive a car but keep stalling it).
3. *Consciously competent.* You know how to do something but still have to concentrate to do it correctly (eg, you have just passed your driving test and can drive, but have to really concentrate not to make mistakes and are still quite nervous).
4. *Unconsciously competent.* You are so skilled that you don't have to think about it anymore (eg, you drive every day but often don't remember paying any attention to driving the car during the journey. Instead you may think about your next team meeting or what you would like to eat for lunch).

So the first step is to work out where you are in the stages of change and then create a specific plan to help you reach the unconsciously competent state.

The aggressive manager

Jonas was a very successful senior manager. However, he believed that he knew best and rarely listened to what his colleagues had to say. Colleagues described his behaviour as aggressive as he regularly raised his voice when giving orders and interrupted staff when they were telling him something.

When asked by a consultant how he would describe his behaviour, Jonas stated that he was a good listener, fair and assertive (*unconsciously incompetent*). However, following a training programme on assertiveness, Jonas was surprised that video evidence of a typical team meeting revealed he spoke loudly, interrupted people and appeared not to listen (*consciously incompetent*). Jonas agreed that this behaviour needed to change, and for the next month made a real effort to interrupt people less and be a better listener. By and large he succeeded, but there was still the occasional 'relapse' into his old behaviour, especially when he felt stressed (*consciously competent*). Eventually, after a couple of months of trying, colleagues really noticed a difference in Jonas's behaviour, and rarely felt he didn't listen to them anymore. Jonas was pleasantly surprised with this feedback, as he rarely thought about how he communicated (*unconsciously competent*).

DIFFERENT APPROACHES TO EI

With the rapid worldwide growth of EI training and literature, it is not surprising that a number of different theories have emerged about what EI actually is.

EI and personality

EI is not another term for personality. Our personalities are relatively fixed, whereas all aspects of EI can be changed. EI is about how we choose to manage the personalities we have. For example, both an extrovert and an introvert may have low levels of personal power, regularly putting themselves into the victim role and blaming others. It would be beneficial for both of these personality types to develop their personal power. So the focus here is on changing attitudes and behaviours, not on changing your personality (and why on earth would anyone want to change their personality in the first place!).

EI and motivation

EI is closely connected to motivation. Taken literally, the word 'motivation' means 'move emotions'. If we have highly developed EI, we have a better understanding of what drives us and triggers positive and negative feelings within us. These positive feelings can be linked to values, attitudes, beliefs, needs, desires, likes and dislikes. For example, let's say you really like mountain climbing because you enjoy the activity itself and you have a belief that mountain climbing is good for you as it will improve your health. If your friend calls and invites you to come climbing with him at the weekend, the mere thought of mountain climbing is likely to trigger positive feelings. Another way of describing this is to say you are motivated to go climbing. Similarly, if you had a bad accident mountain climbing once and developed an attitude that it is a dangerous sport, you may experience negative feelings and thus lack motivation to go along with your friend.

EI and competencies

Some theories of EI view emotional intelligence as a set of competencies that can be learnt simply through training. However, we view EI as an interrelated mix of attitudes that will have an impact on competencies. For example, a training course can teach you how to become a better listener. Taught alone, active listening skills are essentially behaviour training. However, unless you look at your attitudes connected to your regard for and awareness of others, learning how you can listen more actively may not mean that you will do it. Improved listening is likely to happen as a result of developing your regard for and awareness of others, but teaching the competencies to do this alone may not lead to any lasting behaviour change. EI looks at the roots underpinning our behaviour, not just at the surface actions we observe on the outside.

Summary

- Developing your emotional intelligence will improve your performance.
- Everything we do involves thoughts and feelings.
- The triune model of our brain states we have a reptile brain, an unconscious emotional brain (the limbic system) and a thinking brain (pre-frontal cortex).
- Attitudes play a vital role in determining how we feel, think and act.
- Emotional hijacking can occur when our emotions take over our thinking and govern our actions.
- There are two key aspects of emotional intelligence: intrapersonal intelligence (our self-regard and awareness and how well we manage ourselves), and interpersonal intelligence (our regard for and awareness of others and how well we manage our relationships).
- Reflective learning will help you to understand and manage your feelings, attitudes and behaviour more effectively.
- EI is made up of a mixture of attitudes, feelings and thoughts that lead to actions.
- EI can be measured.

- All aspects of EI can be changed.
- Sustainable change takes time as we need to develop from unconsciously incompetent to unconsciously competent.
- Developing your EI will impact on all areas of your life.
- EI is not personality; it is how you choose to manage your personality.
- Developing your EI will help you to understand what motivates you and why.
- Developing competencies alone will not significantly improve your EI.

References

Gallwey, W T (1986) *The Inner Game of Tennis*, Pan, London

Gardner, H (1983/93) *Frames of Mind*, Basic Books, New York

Goleman, D (1996) *Emotional Intelligence: Why it can matter more than IQ*, Bantam Books, London

Griffin, J and Tyrrell, I (2001) *The Human Givens*, Human Givens Publishing, Chalvington

MacLean, P D (1990) *The Triune Brain in Evolution: Role in paleocerebral functions*, Plenum Press, New York

Maddocks, J (2006) *The Brain Science of Emotional Intelligence*, JCA Occupational Psychologists, Cheltenham

Maddocks, J and Sparrow, T (2000) *The Individual and Team Effectiveness Questionnaires*, JCA Occupational Psychologists, Cheltenham

Sparrow, T and Knight, A (2006) *Applied.EI*, Wiley, Chichester

2

What is coaching?

> *You cannot teach a man anything. You can only help him discover it within himself.*
> Galileo Galilei

Imagine having the support of someone who champions your success as much as you do, someone who will ask great questions to encourage you to tap into your own well of resources, to find the solutions you didn't know you had; someone who will challenge you to expand your horizons and see things from different perspectives and viewpoints. That is what EI coaching is all about. Take a look at this scenario.

A new start

Jim is a brand new employee in a high street retailer and is taking on the role of area manager. During his first week, he spends a lot of time with his line manager, Jeff. Jeff talks to Jim about the company, the structure and processes that the company has. He also talks to Jim about his objectives, his development plan and about the specifics of the job. Jim listens a lot of the time, takes plenty of notes and asks questions as they come to mind.

What do you think here – is Jeff coaching Jim? We believe this definitely isn't coaching and yet many organizations talk about coaching employees in this way. While coaching is a very powerful way of helping people develop, it is not the only solution. This example is more like training or mentoring (see later in the chapter for definitions). Let's now consider another scenario.

A problem with sales

Jessica is an Account Director for a training company and she's looking to build on her sales figures. Her boss, Tim, the Sales Director, has a meeting with Jessica about her performance so far this year, and asks her questions about what's happening with her clients and how she feels everything is going. Jessica explains she's concerned as one of her major customers has cut its training budget and so she is below target. Tim listens carefully to what Jessica says and encourages her to explore what is working well, and how she can use this to develop her sales figures further. He asks some great questions that Jessica hasn't thought of before, questions like, 'If you look back at the end of the year having achieved your targets, what will have made this happen for you?', 'If you knew you could only succeed what would you do?', 'What support do you need from your colleagues or me?' By the end of the meeting, Jessica goes away with an action plan she's developed and some great ideas about expanding business with her existing clients. She feels much better about herself and confident about getting the business.

What do you think now? Is this coaching? We'd say a resounding yes. So what's the difference between these two scenarios?

Jim was brand new to the organization and he needed information and knowledge that he had no way of knowing. He needed Jeff to tell him, which was much more of an information giving/mentoring session. If Jeff had asked Jim about the processes and objectives, it wouldn't have worked as he simply wouldn't have known. Coaching isn't the best intervention in this situation; training, telling and mentoring are more appropriate.

Jessica on the other hand knows her job well and it was much more appropriate for Tim to coach and ask questions about what she could do to develop things. Jim had the choice of whether to tell Jessica what to do or coach her to help her find her own solutions. He chose the latter as he knows that Jessica will buy in to her own ideas and solutions quicker and therefore feel confident and more motivated to put them into action.

'What is coaching?' is a question that people have asked for years and no doubt will continue to do so. When we wrote the book, we Googled the word 'coaching' and an astonishing 76,300,000 entries came up. When we looked on Amazon there were around 4,813 resources you can buy; a list that is growing almost daily. That tells us just how big coaching really is. In this chapter, we'll be looking to answer three core questions and we'll be sharing our own extensive experience. We've also tapped into the research that's out there, we've spoken with the main coaching bodies, we've interviewed organizations that are using coaching as part of their people development strategy, and we've interviewed some experts in the coaching field. The key questions we'll be exploring are:

1. What is coaching (and what isn't coaching)?
2. Why coaching?
3. What does great coaching look like?

WHAT IS COACHING?

Coaching is one of *the* most powerful ways of communicating. When used effectively and appropriately it raises your awareness; it's like a laser on your thinking that cuts through any procrastination and straight to the chase. We believe that coaching is about moving forwards and helping people improve their individual performance, which has a knock-on effect for organizations on team and organizational performance. The bottom line is coaching is about being a catalyst for positive change in a way that's appropriate for individuals, helping them to be the very best they can be. Tim Gallwey agrees with our thinking when he says: 'It's about evoking the best from people, including yourself.'

Sir John Whitmore also shares our belief that the purpose of coaching is about raising awareness and responsibility of the person being coached, which ultimately is about assisting them with their progress, productivity and performance. (For the full transcript of the interview with Sir John Whitmore see Appendix 1.)

Unfortunately 'coaching' seems to have become a word that is used to describe all manner of things. It's therefore also important to identify what coaching is not, as it appears to have become 'the answer' for anything to do with change, consultancy and training new people. Let's be clear here, coaching is *not* a panacea for everything! Coaching is not telling someone what to do; it's not giving advice or providing solutions. It is not the same as mentoring, counselling, training or consultancy. However, we firmly believe coaching is hugely powerful when it is delivered by competent, emotionally intelligent coaches in the appropriate circumstances.

The coaching difference

While there are similarities with other interventions such as mentoring, counselling and consultancy, there are also key differences. Let's imagine you are going to bake a cake and you want some input from another person. How might a coach, mentor, counsellor, consultant or trainer help you?

- *A coach* would ask you questions about what end result you want and check if you had everything you needed, what other equipment/ingredients you might need, and check with you that it matched your priorities.
- *A mentor* would share his or her recipe with you and his or her experience of how he or she does it.
- *A counsellor* would explore any anxieties you had about baking the cake.
- *A consultant* would evaluate the situation, provide three or four recipe options and discuss which was appropriate for you.
- *A trainer* would demonstrate how it was done, give you the equipment and ingredients you need, and observe while you were baking it, giving feedback when needed.

Mentoring

We believe that the key difference between coaching and mentoring is that mentors bring their range of expertise, knowledge and experience, which is passed on to the mentee where appropriate. So, if a senior manager is mentoring someone junior to him or her in the organization, he or she is modelling and sharing his or her experiences of what it's like to be doing the job and giving a feel for 'how we do things around here'.

Counselling

Counselling supports people in working through emotional distress or anxieties that prevent them from functioning as well as they'd like to. The counselling conversation can spend a lot of time looking at the past and how people have got to where they are.

Consultancy

Consultants work in organizations in numerous ways, often to define problem areas/inefficiencies and give advice to develop solutions. They bring knowledge and expertise in their areas of work and pass advice on to their clients. Coaching is not about giving advice, though helping coachees really access their own expertise is a key part of it.

Training

Great training is about equipping people with new skills and knowledge to help their personal and/or professional development. The skilled trainer will train/teach people the relevant new information and, ideally (but unfortunately from our experience, rarely) address all four KASH aspects of their subject area (Knowledge, Attitudes, Skills and Habits). Coaching is not about training someone to do something brand new but it is a great way to support teaching/training to really embed the learning, as highlighted by the following research.

Olivero *et al* (1997) looked at the effects of executive coaching with a group of 31 managers. This group had management development training and they measured that their productivity had increased by 22.4 per cent afterwards. When they followed up the training with some coaching, the productivity rose to 88 per cent – a further improvement of more than 65 per cent. This shows just how important coaching can be to make sure that knowledge and skills acquired during training are actually applied back in the workplace.

Activity: Quick check

From the definitions we just gave you (coaching, mentoring, counselling, consulting, and training), what interventions do you feel would be appropriate in each of these situations?

1. A new employee joins an organization and is on his or her first day at work.
2. A manager conducting appraisals with his or her team.
3. A graduate who has identified that he or she would like to work towards being operations manager.
4. A team member who's been off work with depression.
5. An employee who wants to learn about presentation skills.

Answers: it obviously depends on the individual first and foremost. As a general guide we'd recommend:

1. Training/mentoring.
2. Coaching/mentoring.
3. Mentoring/coaching.
4. Possibly counselling (maybe psychotherapy in extreme circumstances).
5. Training. We re-emphasize here that coaching is not a panacea for everything.

Directive or non-directive, that is the question

There are different schools of thought about whether coaching is directive or non-directive. We believe that non-directive coaching is hugely effective, as individuals are the experts in their life and they're far more likely to put their own ideas into action, rather than when they're being told what to do.

While coaching may be non-directive, it is without doubt directional, as it is about moving forwards and the coach will ensure the direction stays on track, according to what the coachee wants to achieve. Above all, coaching is about being appropriate for the individual. As a coach you will have an impact on the coaching session as you're unique and have a unique set of values, attitudes and beliefs that will make a difference to how you listen and the types of questions you ask. It is not about you being 'an empty vessel' but is about bringing the essence of you to the coaching relationship (and not your content).

Sir John Whitmore agrees and maintains, 'it is a myth to say the coach is a vacuum and works entirely on the other person's agenda, because you as a coach alter the context merely by your presence with another human being'.

Imagine a ladder that represents the different styles of communication, with the top rungs of the ladder being non-directive and the bottom being directive. The higher up the ladder you are, the more input, ownership and responsibility there is from the coachee. The lower down the ladder you are, the more input there is from the communicator (be it a coach, mentor, consultant, or trainer). It would look something like Figure 2.1.

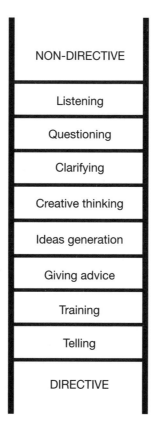

Figure 2.1 The coaching ladder

Remembering the primary purpose of coaching is to raise awareness, encourage responsibility and facilitate change, more of this takes place higher up the ladder. The top of the ladder is where pure non-directive coaching takes place, using highly tuned listening, great questioning and clarity seeking. A consultant or trainer would communicate up and down the whole ladder, using listening skills through to telling others what to do. A mentor would certainly be up to at least midway on the rungs of the ladder. Again, it is about what is appropriate for the person and situation. For leaders or managers it is often more of a challenge to operate at the top of the ladder as they are used to problem solving, giving solutions and telling people what to do. Leaders who embrace non-directive coaching as a practised skill will reap the rewards of seeing an improvement in the progress, productivity and performance of themselves, their team and the organization. They will know when and how to use it to best effect and when purely telling people, advising or mentoring them is appropriate. Richard Branson is certainly recognized as being such a leader.

The manager who gets it wrong

Dominic works for a large pharmaceutical company. He goes on a one-day course about coaching and decides to use it 'on his staff'. What Dominic does is go back to work and tell his team he'll be coaching them to get their work done. Dominic first of all decides to use it with Richard, who's a brand new recruit to the company. He tells Richard about the company, the department, his new job and what needs to be done. After spending an hour or two 'coaching' Richard, Dominic goes to a team meeting and he 'coaches' them to solve a couple of key challenges by giving his opinion of what should be done and then asking who is going to do it. Next Dominic calls a meeting with Paul who is underperforming and Dominic decides to 'coach' him to help get Paul out of the business.

How effective is Dominic as a coach? Not very! He quite simply is not a coach, but believes he now has the skills to be one. It is not appropriate to use coaching for someone who's brand new to a company, when it's new knowledge and/or skills he or she needs. It is also not appropriate to wrap coaching up as a way to get what *you* want implemented or to manage poor performance. The latter examples were more about manipulation. The intention of the coach is hugely important to the effectiveness of coaching. It must be about genuinely wanting to help, support, encourage and champion the other person to move forward.

Thinking about the KASH model, coaching is definitely appropriate for supporting a change in attitudes and behaviours. Coaching does not work for people who need brand new knowledge and skills right now, unless they have negative attitudes connected to that new knowledge or skills training, eg 'I don't want to go but I have been told to' or, 'I'm not good enough to do this.' However, it can work well for running alongside training/mentoring to really embed new skills and knowledge. We saw this in the research we mentioned earlier about the company that ran a training programme for its managers and measured the increase in productivity, and then topped up the training with coaching and again measured the increase in productivity. The difference the coaching made was over 65 per cent more in productivity terms.

Activity

If you are looking to coach others or be coached, ask yourself these questions and be really honest with yourself, because it does make a difference as to whether coaching will be effective or not.

Your readiness to coach – five key questions

1. Do you have a genuine regard for and interest in others?
2. Do you have a high level of self-regard?
3. Are you open to suspending your own judgements and assumptions and keeping your own agenda out of a coaching conversation?
4. Do you regularly listen to your own feelings and check how they affect your behaviour?
5. Are you open to learning the necessary skills and committing to ongoing learning and development to broaden your view of the world?

NB: in Chapter 5 there are more detailed questionnaires for you to complete about regard and awareness levels.

Your readiness to be coached – five key questions

1. Are you looking to make changes?
2. Are you ready to take responsibility for where you are and where you want to move to?
3. Are you open to challenge and fresh perspectives?
4. Are you ready to be the best you can be and not to sabotage yourself in any way?
5. Are you willing to be different and take the action that is necessary?

WHY COACHING?

Coaching is one of the fastest growing means of people development. Why? Because it gets results and helps improve performance and productivity, providing it is used effectively. There has been a lot of research carried out into the effectiveness of coaching and the benefits it brings, and we'll be referring to some of this here as well as hearing what two major organizations feel are the key benefits it's brought to them. CIPD (Chartered Institute of Personnel and Development) in the UK has done some research on the use of coaching and in fact 92 per cent of the organizations they interviewed are using it!

Coaching not only impacts productivity, it can also positively affect:

- confidence and motivation;
- behaviour change;
- culture; and
- leadership.

So does coaching really work?

In the book *The Case for Coaching*, the authors did some research with multiple organizations that have used coaching in the workplace. Ninety-six per cent of respondents claimed that coaching has had a positive impact on individual performance, and 87 per cent of respondents said that coaching has had a positive impact on organizational performance.

CIPD observed the following benefits to organizations:

- improved individual performance;
- improved productivity;
- increased staff motivation;
- accelerated change in organizations;
- demonstrated the organization's commitment to staff;
- improved staff retention;
- reduced cost of sending staff to external courses;
- growth of future senior staff;
- fostered a culture of learning and development;
- helped staff to achieve a better work-life balance.

Dr Patrick Williams, in response to the 'Why coaching?' question, feels that in the biggest sense, coaching can be transformational. He maintains that coaching gives an opportunity for people to say and think things out loud that they've probably never said to an objective listener. (For our interview with Dr Williams, see Appendix 2.)

Is there a case for coaching in organizations?

The fact that most large organizations today include coaching in one form or another in their people development strategy says it all. The research into this growing industry shows evidence that there is indeed a case for coaching in general. As we've already discussed, coaching is not a panacea for everything. How successful it will be for your organization depends on several factors, which we look at in the next chapter.

Putting forward the case for coaching

So you think coaching is an ideal component to support the growth of your organization. What now? Once you've considered the points above, then it's time to move on to the practical elements and put together a case to present to your board for consideration.

Let's take an example of what a company did to present its case for coaching. While you're reading this, look out for the seven-step process we use to help organizations decide on the viability of coaching.

Introducing coaching

James, an HR Director of a healthcare company, had experience of coaching with his last job and he was keen to introduce it to his new company, starting with the senior management team. He believed his responsibility was managing the organization's best asset, its people, and while the organization's growth had slowed down in recent months, he knew there was a huge amount of potential to really bring out. James believed that coaching could make the difference.

He knew that his first job was to put a case forward for it, so he put a proposal document together, covering some key points. This included the key aims and intention of what he wanted to achieve (implementing the people side of the company strategy). James defined coaching, why he felt it could support the business and how, backed up by the evidence from research and the business benefits. He explored other options in the proposal and the impact of not using coaching. Next came information on the proposed coaching programme and the practicalities (the format, the numbers to be coached, the objectives to be achieved, the primary focus, and who would be delivering the coaching – internal or external coaches). James wrote about the various ways the company could evaluate the coaching and attached a summary. The final part was looking at the options and next steps (such as run a pilot programme, do nothing until a meeting or presentation, research further before any decisions are made).

How did you get on with identifying the seven key steps? Here they are:

1. Decide on the framework of your proposal document and define what you want to achieve.
2. Define coaching and why you feel it could benefit the business (you may want to include the cost of not implementing coaching as well as other options you've considered, such as a leadership development programme).
3. Outline the business benefits and refer to any relevant research to provide evidence for your plans.
4. Put forward a proposed coaching strategy/programme and the practicalities (format, numbers to receive coaching, where it would take place, how often).
5. Define the resources that would be needed, the time taken, investment of the coaching, cost of time away from the business, materials, etc).
6. Offer alternative ways of measuring the success of the programme and include the resources needed to do the evaluation (time and money).
7. Summary and recommended next steps.

Our process is backed up by the steps outlined by the CIPD (2004). Sir John Whitmore agrees with our views when he says:

> The business case is about performance and staff satisfaction, which really is a major issue. If staff are treated in a command and control way, they probably don't enjoy being at work. Staff retention of the top talent is so important to organizations and so a coaching management style is ideal. This doesn't mean people are all qualified coaches, but that they manage in a coaching way.

What role does coaching play for individuals, organizations and society?

Imagine individuals who work with a coach who supports and encourages them to raise their game and be the very best version of themselves. Those individuals become clearer about what they want, the direction they're going in, are more motivated and energized to grow and take action to move themselves forward and achieve more than they thought they could. Now imagine a team of people working together who have the same kind of support, and then an entire organization. The role that coaching could have is massive.

Coaching is a profession that is growing at a pace and, therefore, the role coaching plays will undoubtedly expand and develop. Coaching is about facilitating change, which could be anything from an individual who is looking to progress his or her career right through to an organization wishing to go through a culture change process. Some coaches specialize in youth coaching, some in life coaching and some in coaching executives. Whatever type of coaching, it can have a massive positive effect on individuals, teams, organizations and ultimately society.

In organizations, flatter leaner structures mean that people have more responsibilities and greater pressures than before. Coaching can be a great tool for helping managers to deal with change, conflict, achieving aims and objectives and working with their people as individuals. Attracting and retaining good people is at the top of most corporate agendas and coaching could make the difference, and demonstrate that you really do value your people for who they are as well as what they do. Also, as we mentioned in Chapter 1, the KASH model of development requires that attitudes and habits are challenged and changed if true, lasting developments are to take place. Often coaching is the ideal way to do this.

Kirsten Poulsen of EMCC agrees that coaching plays an important role and she says:

> I think the reason coaching is very hot and popular is that we are an individualistic society, everybody would like to realize and actualize their power and have a great life, where people are loyal to themselves a bit more than maybe to companies. This requires managers to be more aware of individuals and to become more a leader than a manager.

(For our full interview with Kirsten Poulsen, President of EMCC, Denmark, see Appendix 4.)

The impact of great coaching – two case studies

We've interviewed people from two organizations that have implemented coaching in their workplace, to demonstrate the positive impact coaching can have.

1: Gasco, Abu Dhabi – Ged Palmer, Organizational Capability Division

Gasco is part of the ADNOC Group (Abu Dhabi National Oil Corporation) which employs about 20,000 people. Here Ged Palmer of the Organizational Capability Division shares Gasco's experiences of providing coaching skills development for its middle managers.

What does your coaching initiative look like?

Our programme is for first and second line managers who manage our graduates. It is three days' training plus a one-to-one coaching follow-up session, one month after the course, then two months after the course.

What has been the impact so far?

The impact has been very strong, though initially there was some misunderstanding. The expectation was it was going to train them to be trainers/instructors. Taking responsibility was a whole new ball game for them. The feedback has been fantastic, the impact is getting bigger and there is momentum with managers asking how they can get on the programme. We're now running programmes every two to three months and there's a good perception internally about them.

Have you measured the impact?

Not specifically but we have evaluated it. There have been some notable individual successes, cases we've collected in our follow-ups. There've been breakthroughs in terms of managers and their graduates. We had people who weren't performing and we have a system of monitoring their progress (a flag system that is very structured). If they have a red flag that means they are behind on their progress. The coaching has engaged them and increased motivation.

Can you give any examples?

Yes. A mechanical engineer was not responding to or getting involved with work activities. After the programme, equipped with new tools, his supervisor had noticed what motivated him and placed him on a project that fitted with his interest/personal motivators, working with engines on site. The coaching has helped to dramatically improve his performance and productivity – his self-esteem has built up and rapport with colleagues has built up – he's now become a star of the team and a green flag rather than a red flag category.

What else have you noticed in terms of impact or measurement?

An indirect measure is the commitment of people, and looking at how people are using coaching; an interesting spin off benefit is how it's helping them with work-life balance or family issues. It's also improving communication and helping with career development and planning for retirement. Some graduates have also commented on the positive changes in their supervisors. Graduate retention has improved and motivation has improved.

What has made the coaching so successful?

Management support and commitment to the project from day one, especially the development manager and the senior management team. The course design is another important factor. The one-to-ones have been fantastic and we are now getting other development courses (supervisor programmes) embedded by one-to-one coaching as this has been so successful. The follow-ups help them to experience the coaching themselves and are a great reminder of what great coaching is. (For the full interview with Ged Palmer of Gasco see www.ei-coachtraining.com/interviews)

2: Audrey Oliphant, Coaching Consultant of Royal Bank of Scotland, Dealer Finance

The Royal Bank of Scotland provides training for its car dealer clients (the Dealer Finance division) and has introduced coaching-based sales training programmes together with one-to-one coaching to embed the training. Here, we interview Audrey about it.

Tell us about the background to the project

We provide a service to our customers, car dealers that use our finance, and we train their managers to increase their performance financially. We offer a Sales Manager Programme (sales with a coaching style) for the motor industry, which is a 10-day course. In between the modules a coach visits the learner for a half-day session (the whole programme is accredited by the Institute of the Motor Industry). Each person has a pre-course visit and then four follow-up coaching sessions, with the last session involving the line manager for evaluation purposes. The participants complete action plans throughout the programme.

What was the business need for the training and coaching?

To support our client group and for the bank to achieve its KPIs by penetrating a target market (car industry).

What has been the impact of the programme?

The programme helped the clients achieve direction, improve sales, develop leadership skills. A common comment was 'the coaching has helped me get in my head and see things from different angles'.

How have you measured the programme?

At the pre-session we identified goals and areas to work on. As much as possible we identified financial gains, such as increase of £100 profit from each sale, 30 per cent up on profits, etc.

Audrey put us in contact with Richard Symes, Fleet and Commercial Sales Manager at a Peugeot car dealership. He described the impact to us. 'Six months ago I was a sales manager. Now I am a sales coach and my department's performance is all the better for it. This change came with the realization that one cannot continue doing the same things hoping that next time the outcome will be better. To achieve a different result, you have to work to a different set of procedures.

'The follow-up visits of my coach were invaluable. The process allowed me to consider all options and make the right decisions. I now believe sales managers should focus more on "people work" – they should be coaches. Recruiting and training new staff is, in my book, far more expensive and time-consuming than ongoing training of existing personnel.'

(To see the full interview with Audrey Oliphant, visit www.ei-coachtraining.com/interviews)

WHAT DOES GREAT COACHING LOOK LIKE?

To answer this question, let's first of all look at when coaching doesn't work and how it is sometimes misused in organizations.

We believe coaching won't work if the coach does not have the right skill level, the right attitude towards the coachee and/or him- or herself. It won't work if the person being coached resists it and has no intention of changing, or when he or she is emotionally stuck and unable to move forwards. It does not work when it's forced. The client/coachee has to be in the right place for coaching.

Tim Gallwey talks about how coaching will not work when the coach doesn't really care, when he or she takes over the burden of the problem or the issue and when there is a judgemental atmosphere. He also mentions when the coachee feels too much self-doubt, inadequacy or fear of failure or judgement, then it won't work. (To see what else Tim Gallwey says about coaching, see our interview in Appendix 3.) In Chapter 3 we explore the three main reasons why coaching doesn't work.

In what ways do some organizations misuse coaching?

In our experience some organizations use coaching as a way to wrap up poor performance management, to get people out of the business, which we feel is unethical. Coaching is not a quick fix to 'sort people out' as we've been requested to do from time to time (needless to say we've turned down the requests). Another common theme is companies wanting their managers to be coaches and not equipping them properly.

Organizations need to be clear about why they're introducing coaching and then communicate it clearly to their managers and employees (whoever is being affected by the intervention). If you are training managers to become coaches, and are expecting to see changes in behaviours, you need to allow adequate time for them to be trained and to experience coaching. You also need to be clear about what you expect from these managers after the training. For example, if it is to hold one-to-ones with their direct subordinates through coaching, then this needs to be communicated to the potential coaches.

The effective coach

Jane is a qualified coach who is continually expanding her knowledge and skills of coaching and the world in general. She has high self-regard and regard for others, and is forever checking in with her self-awareness, through using a learning log of her coaching activities and how she feels about it, as well as working with her coaching supervisor. This is the ideal scenario as far as great emotionally intelligent coaching is concerned.

So, what does it take to be a great coach? We believe great coaches are people who:

- are emotionally intelligent (more about this in Chapter 3);
- take an interest in the world around them;
- have great integrity and strong ethics;
- care about other people and appreciate the precious gemstones that are inside them, knowing others are totally capable and resourceful;
- know their own boundaries and respect those of others and are constantly developing themselves;
- are genuinely curious and interested in others and who are non-judgemental and can put to one side any assumptions they may have;
- facilitate change through being engaging communicators;
- build relationships well, listen attentively, ask great laser questions;
- are tuned in to their intuition like their own internal satellite navigation system;
- encourage new viewpoints and have a natural positive energy about them.

When asked about what it takes to be a great coach, Sir John Whitmore maintains that:

> being a great coach takes practice, with awareness. You could drive 100,000 miles a year and not get any better, if you don't do it with awareness. As a coach you could coach 100 people and not get any better too, unless you pay a lot of attention to what you're doing and how it is received.

What's the secret ingredient for great coaching?

You won't be surprised to know that for us one of the absolute key ingredients for great coaching is emotional intelligence. When coaches value themselves and others, are extremely self-aware and tuned into others at the same time, then you have the makings of great coaching. It's about a coach's presence and energy, which creates the right environment for positive changes to take place. The brilliance of coaching takes place when the coach is fully present and doesn't need to know the answers.

WHAT NEXT? WHAT DOES THE FUTURE OF COACHING LOOK LIKE?

Coaching is without doubt here to stay and is not a passing fad! We believe the future is definitely bright and the possibilities are endless. Coaching can have a huge impact on all walks of life, from education, developing young people's development, developing the three Ps at work (progress, productivity and performance), deeper conversations and understanding of partners, friends and family, helping people with retirement, and the list continues. We think (and hope) that more organizations will embrace a coaching style of leadership and use it appropriately.

While the profession is not regulated, there is more of a move towards self-regulation, and several key professional bodies are developing the standards of this growth industry. We believe there'll be more internal coaches developed and the job market will see the posts of 'coaches' for organizations increasing. The number of training courses for coaches is increasing dramatically as well, and the ICF and the EMCC have a process where they accredit/recognize training providers.

Summary

- Coaching is without doubt one of the fastest growing areas of people development.
- Research shows that with quality coaching, there are numerous benefits to individuals, organizations and ultimately society.
- Coaching is definitely here to stay and has a huge role to play in the way people communicate, interact and develop.
- Coaching is a process, a tool, an emerging profession, an industry in its infancy and above all, a way of communicating.
- Coaching is not a panacea for everything and beware any organization or individual who tells you that it is.
- While there are similarities, there are also distinct differences between coaching and mentoring, counselling, psychotherapy, training and consultancy.
- There is a big difference between average and outstanding coaches.
- Emotional Intelligence makes a difference to the quality of coaching (see the next chapter).
- Coaching is about being appropriate in the moment to match the requirements of the coachee.
- There is a clear business case for coaching.

- The future of coaching looks set for substantial growth; at the time of writing it is estimated there are approximately 50,000 coaches worldwide.
- While coaching is not regulated there are more professional bodies that are looking to set and maintain the high standards of the industry, eg ICF, EMCC and the Association for Coaching.

References

CIPD (2004) *Buying Coaching Services Research Paper,* CIPD, London

Downey, M (2002 and 2003) *Effective Coaching,* Texere, London

Jarvis, L and Fillery-Travis, A (2006) *The Case for Coaching,* CIPD, London

Olivero, G B, Bane, K D and Kopelman, R E (1997) Executive coaching as a transfer of training tool: effects on productivity in a public agency, *Personnel Management,* **26** (4) pp 461–9

Passmore, J (2007) *Excellence in Coaching,* Kogan Page, London

Whitmore, J (2002) *Coaching for Performance,* Nicholas Brearley, London

Whitworth, L, Kimsey-House, H and Sandahl, P (1998) *Co-Active Coaching,* Davies-Black, California

Wilson, C (2007) *Best Practice in Performance Coaching,* Kogan Page, London

3

The importance of emotional intelligence in coaching

Asking someone who is not emotionally intelligent to coach others is like sending a newly qualified driver out on the roads in a Formula 1 car.

WHAT'S WRONG WITH COACHING?

Coaching is growing rapidly. As we mentioned in Chapter 2, a recent survey by the Chartered Institute of Personnel and Development revealed that:

- 96 per cent of business people believe coaching can benefit organizations;
- 92 per cent of business people believe coaching improves an organization's bottom line;
- 88 per cent of line managers are coaching staff;
- 64 per cent of organizations use external coaches.

To meet this demand, more and more companies are offering coach training opportunities, ranging from 12-month Diploma courses, to one- or two-day programmes claiming to teach people the essential coaching skills to be able to go and coach others. Whilst this increased recognition that coaching can have benefits to individuals and companies is encouraging, the rapid growth of coaching brings with it many hidden dangers.

In Chapter 2 we looked at the many different definitions and interpretations of coaching that exist. Here we will look at the vital role emotional intelligence plays in the success of coaching, both for the coach and the person being coached.

Warning: not all managers can coach!

One worrying thing about coaching is the number of managers who are now being asked to coach without having undergone sufficient self-development themselves. Being coached by someone who is emotionally unintelligent is dangerous. Apart from damaging the reputation and understanding of coaching, it can prove harmful to both the individual being coached and the coach. The following example demonstrates this point.

Kate the reluctant coach

Kate was a directive manager who liked to control her staff. She believed that a manager's role was to take charge of staff, always being the strongest figure and knowing more than those you are managing. Kate's organization had recently started a culture change and, as part of this change, all managers had been told to attend a two-day coaching course to equip them to start a monthly coaching session with their subordinates. The course focused mainly on empathy, listening and questioning skills, all of which Kate felt she knew already. On returning to work, Kate arranged to coach one of her team, Diana. Going straight into the coaching session with her old belief that a manager must always know more than the people she manages, she soon became frustrated with asking open questions. This was made worse by the fact that Diana seemed reluctant to open up in the session and it seemed to be going nowhere. This resulted in Kate resorting to her old habit of telling people what to do. The session ended with Kate giving Diana three actions to take away and report back on in the next coaching session.

So what went wrong? It may be easier to ask what went right here! The whole situation was set up to fail right from the start. Here are just some of the things that could have contributed to this coaching failure:

- As a directive, controlling manager, Kate shows a higher regard for herself than for others. Just because she has been told she needs to develop a coaching style of management does not mean this attitude will change.
- Kate had a negative attitude to attending the training. 'This is a waste of two valuable days – I already know how to listen and ask questions.' As a result she was closed to any new ideas and didn't really learn anything.

■ The training course focused on only some useful coaching skills. As we saw in Chapter 1, any training that does not use the KASH approach (Knowledge, Attitudes, Skills and Habits) is in danger of failing. Here, the main issue is Kate's attitudes, not her skills, so focusing on skills for two days will change little.

■ It is unrealistic for the organization to think that a manager can train to be a successful coach in just two days. Coaching is a highly skilled profession, requiring months of training and a coach with a highly developed emotional intelligence.

■ Diana was reluctant to open up in the session. This is not surprising as she did not like Kate's normal directive style of leadership and felt that any honesty she showed could be seen as a weakness and used against her. This was made worse by the fact that Kate did not set boundaries around the coaching, with clear guidelines on reporting and confidentiality. Perhaps even more fundamental, nobody asked Diana if she wanted to be coached! You cannot coach anyone who does not want to enter into a coaching relationship.

■ The organizational culture was not supportive of coaching. Generally, levels of trust and motivation were low and most staff feared for their jobs, given that yet more changes were on the way. Diana viewed the coaching as a deceptive way of finding out who would be made redundant when the changes come.

Introducing coaching into a company culture often does not succeed. In summary, there are three basic requirements for successful coaching:

1. The coach needs to be emotionally intelligent and have the necessary coaching knowledge, skills, attitudes and habits.
2. The person being coached must want to be coached and be ready to change.
3. The organization where the coaching takes place needs to have a culture suitable for coaching.

Activity: How successful is coaching in your organization?

Take a moment to consider how successful coaching has been in your organization. Using the above three requirements as general categories, ask yourself the following questions:

1. *The coach needs to be emotionally intelligent and skilled.*
    Are all the coaches who work in your organization emotionally intelligent? Do they have highly developed self-regard, or do any of them seem to show an 'I'm ok as long as I help others' attitude, reacting strongly if the coaching does not seem to work?
    Are the coaches genuinely showing a high regard for others, going into the coaching relationship with the intention of helping the person being coached to in some way benefit from the coaching?
    Do the coaches your organization uses 'empty themselves' of strong emotions before coaching and show high levels of emotional control during the coaching sessions?
    Are the coaches you use highly attuned to the people they coach, showing high levels of empathy and paying careful attention to visual cues, voice changes, the type of words people use and emotional responses?

2. *The person being coached must want to be coached and be ready to change.*
    Are open discussions used to explain what coaching is and how it can be used, and to determine the attitudes towards coaching of the person being coached?
    Does the coach listen carefully for words or phrases suggesting reluctance to change and low personal power? Phrases like 'I have to', 'I need to', 'I should', 'I suppose I could', and 'I might' all suggest some reluctance or lack of motivation to change.
    Are regular reviews and evaluations of the effectiveness of the coaching used to determine what the person being coached thinks about it?

3. *The organization where the coaching takes place needs to have a culture suitable for coaching.*
    What changes have recently taken place in your organization and how have they impacted staff morale?
    What are the absenteeism and staff turnover rates?
    How much are staff willing to put in extra time and effort for the benefit of the organization?
    Are clear boundaries and contracts put in place around coaching, covering things like confidentiality, frequency, purpose of coaching and measurement?

For the rest of this chapter, we will look at what makes an emotionally intelligent coach, focusing on the four foundations of becoming a successful coach: self-regard, regard for others, self-awareness and awareness of others. In Chapter 5 we will look at a number of practical tools for self-development in these four areas.

THE EMOTIONALLY INTELLIGENT COACH

In his studies on leadership, Daniel Goleman has identified six different leadership styles, one of which is coaching. Having managers who can coach is recognized by more and more companies as an essential requirement for successful people management. In business in the future a coaching style of leadership could become so universal that it is just the normal way people manage others.

However, asking someone who is emotionally unintelligent to coach others is a bit like asking someone who has just passed their driving test to take a Formula 1 car out on the road. Many organizations assume that their managers should coach others because they know more about the technical aspects of the job, and that's why they became managers in the first place. Applying this false belief to a coaching situation is potentially a big mistake.

As we saw in Chapter 1, technical knowledge only accounts for about 15 per cent of your success. Far more important for successful coaching is the human engineering aspect: how well you manage yourself and how effective you are at managing relationships with others. To be a truly effective coach, an individual needs to have a high level of emotional intelligence combined with the right knowledge, skills and experience of coaching others. This combination will produce an EI coach, an authentic coach who helps coachees to change and develop their performance.

In our view, it is both immoral and ineffective to ask someone who has not sufficiently developed his or her own levels of emotional intelligence to coach others. Using the first four scales of emotional intelligence to support this claim, we will now look at why having a high EI is vital to being a successful coach.

LIFE POSITIONS: THE FOUNDATIONS TO SUCCESSFUL COACHING

The starting point for developing your EI and becoming a successful coach is the core attitudes you have about yourself and others. These two life positions are your self-regard (how ok you believe you are) and your regard for others (how ok you believe others are).

Self-regard (self-esteem)

You can't really help others until you have helped yourself!

Developing your own EI and becoming a successful coach start with your own self-regard. If you truly value yourself for who you are, not just what you do, then you will be more inclined to truly respect others and less likely to judge them. There is no easy recipe to improving your self-esteem – it takes time, willpower, focus, effort and patience. Much of your self-esteem will have been defined during your childhood, where you came into the world wanting to be loved and desperately seeking love and reassurance from those who cared for you.

Unfortunately, many of us develop a self-regard based on conditions. For example, if you had a parent who only praised you when you achieved good grades at school, you may have developed a conditional self-regard attitude of, 'I am ok as long as I am successful.' Unless challenged, this conditional belief will stay with you during adulthood, leading to disappointment and self-doubt when you are not successful (this will inevitably happen sometimes). A much healthier attitude could be, 'I am ok irrespective of whether I succeed. It is good to be successful but it does not make me a less valuable person if I don't always succeed.'

Conditional self-regard is something most of us develop as a way of accepting and valuing ourselves. The problem is that there is always the possibility of the condition failing to be met, thus leading to disappointment and feelings of low self-worth. Some common examples of conditional self-regard are:

'I am ok as long as I'm perfect.'
'I am ok as long as I win.'
'I am ok as long as I earn lots of money.'
'I am ok as long as I am busy.'
'I am ok as long as I have lots of friends.'
'I am ok as long as I help others.'

Activity

It might be worth taking a moment to work out your own conditions you attach to your self-regard. Make a list of the conditions you put on yourself that, in your mind, make you ok as a person.

I am ok because I am me

So, what would it take for you to believe the statement above? It may sound simple, but to genuinely think and feel this is a very powerful thing. It will provide you with a foundation to develop other areas of your emotional intelligence, not least how much you respect others, coach others and behave in a trustworthy, reliable way yourself.

There are many things you can do to improve your self-esteem (but there is no quick fix!) We will look at some concrete activities more extensively in Chapter 5.

How does this relate to coaching?

Being able to separate who you are and what you do is vital for a coach (and anybody who is not a coach!) Many people who are attracted to a profession of helping others such as coaching, may choose to do this because they have a need to help others as this is confused with their self-regard. In other words, they have a conditional self-regard: 'I am ok as long as I help others.' Another common conditional self-regard often connected to managers is: 'I am ok as long as I am in control.' Having either of these unconscious attitudes, both of which stem from low self-regard, is likely to lead to ineffective coaching or managing.

All too frequently, we find ourselves making moral judgements of others if our own self-regard is not sufficiently developed. We say things to ourselves such as, 'I don't like you', 'You are stupid' or, 'You are not worth coaching.' Statements like these are emotionally unintelligent, because they are coming from an 'I'm ok, you're not ok' position. During recent coach training with a team of top managers, one of them told us about the problems he had working with one particular person. 'I find it really difficult working with this idiot. He is so judgemental and never listens to anything I say.' Can you spot the irony in this statement? By thinking of the person as an 'idiot' the trainee was coming from an 'I'm ok, you're not ok' position, which is making a moral judgement of the other person. There's an old saying that 'Two wrongs don't make a right', which seems to fit quite well here. We are more likely to judge others if our own self-regard is low. Often people with low self-regard will:

- be critical;
- be judgemental;
- blame others;
- be mistrustful.

To be an effective, non-directive coach and to be able to separate what you do from who you are, you need to have high self-esteem. In other words, if you are coaching more for your own needs rather than the needs of the coachee, it is a dangerous place to be, for both of you.

Don't make coaching into a drama

The fact that some coaches coach others more for their own needs rather than the needs of their coachees can be explained by the Karpman Drama Triangle model, developed by Stephen Karpman; see Figure 3.1.

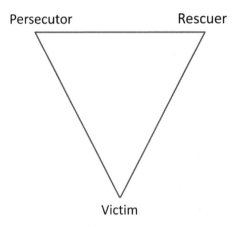

Figure 3.1   The Karpman triangle

This model describes how we can sometimes take on the role of helper/rescuer, persecutor or victim. Awareness of these roles is essential in coaching, as is knowing where to draw boundaries in the coaching relationship.

When a person comes to a coach it is usually because he or she wants support, which means different things to different people. As an EI coach it is important to be aware and recognize if the coachee is in victim role. If a coach isn't emotionally intelligent, he or she can unconsciously take on the role of helper or persecutor, neither of which is a healthy place to be. The coach, at all times, needs to be aware of the boundaries and ensure he or she does not step over the mark in terms of the support he or she is offering.

How is this linked with self-regard? A coach with low self-regard may have the condition of worth, 'I am ok as long as I am a successful coach.' This condition means coaches are more likely to go beyond the boundaries in their coaching, always going the extra mile for their coachee because they need to help others to feel ok about themselves. This might mean allowing sessions to run on, allowing the coachee to call them anytime, becoming too emotionally involved with the coachee, or other small things that go outside of normal coaching boundaries. This is a dangerous place to be. Let's say the coachee may still not be satisfied and may move into the role of persecutor – blaming the coach for his or her lack of progress and perhaps even telling friends what a bad experience he or she had with this coach. What happens to the coach now? Typically, as his or her self-esteem has been hurt ('I am not ok because I am not a good coach'), he or she moves into the role of victim, maybe even going and finding a helper, telling them what a terrible coachee he or she had.

As we said earlier, it is essential that practising coaches have high self-esteem and have the ability to remove themselves from what they are doing. As we are all human and all of us will experience periods where our self-esteem is lower, high self-awareness is also essential. It is therefore a good idea to employ a coach supervisor, as this is something that can be regularly discussed in supervision. Indeed, one of the most powerful questions we can reflect on after a session is, 'Who did I ask that question for – me or my coachee?' We will look more at the role supervision plays in the chapter on ethics.

Regard for others

In order to be an authentic coach, high regard for others is also essential. If you have a high regard for others then you accept them for who they are and are less likely to start judging them. Judgement is the enemy of any coach, because it clouds understanding and leads to directive coaching on the coach's terms. For example, let's say a coachee tells you about something you disapprove of, such as lying to his or her manager. It is important as a coach to remember that even though you may not approve, your coachee is not a bad person for doing this. High regard for others is about accepting that other people have the right to do what they do simply because they are them. This doesn't mean you have to agree with everything they do, but it does mean that your place as a non-directive coach is to be aware of your own beliefs and values and keep them out of the coaching session. For example, with lying to a manager, a judgemental coach might believe this is wrong and therefore start 'interrogating' the coachee: 'Why did you do that?', 'What do you think is wrong about lying?' This is clearly not showing regard for others. On the other hand, having high regard for others means accepting what the coachee has told you and remaining non-directive in your questioning: 'How do you feel about this?' It is important to remember, however, that all coaches are human. There may be times when the coach's values clash significantly with those of the individual or organization he or she is working with, and then it is best not to start or to choose to terminate the coaching.

The following extract from a dialogue between a coach and her coachee demonstrates how allowing your own judgement of others can impact on coaching:

Coach (Charlotte): So what would you like to talk about today?
Coachee: One of the women on my team, she is proving difficult to work with.

Coach: What exactly is the problem?

Coachee: She never does what I ask her and this is putting extra pressure on me.

Coach: What do you think the reason is?

Coachee: I hate to say it, but I think it's because she's a woman.

Coach: What do you mean?

Coachee: Well, women are scattier than men and often promise things they can't deliver.

Coach: What's wrong with this belief you have?

Coachee: What's wrong with it? (pause) Well, I don't think there is anything wrong with it, it's just the way it is.

Coach: How can you change this belief?

Coachee: I don't want to change it, I just want a more reliable colleague.

Coach: If you don't want to change, how can coaching help you?

Hopefully you can spot where the coach clearly starts allowing her own judgements to impact on the session. It is quite possible that Charlotte believes that her coachee is wrong to brand all women as 'scatty', and she probably has some form of emotional reaction to hearing her coachee say this. This is perfectly acceptable as she is a human being with her own values and will not always agree with everything her coachees say. However, rather than staying in the 'I'm ok, you're ok' position, she appears to move into an 'I'm ok, you're not ok' judgemental position. By asking her coachee what is wrong with this belief about women, she is allowing her own judgement to seep into the session. Nobody likes being judged, so not surprisingly her coachee does not respond positively to this question.

How can this be prevented? To prevent their own values from seeping into a coaching session, coaches must have both a high regard for others and a high self-awareness, noticing when they have an emotional response to a statement and not allowing this 'emotional hijack' to take over their thoughts and actions.

Everybody is ok!

The theory of transactional analysis combines these core attitudes of self-regard and regard for others in four life positions, often referred to as 'the ok corral' (see Figure 3.2). We will now describe these four positions and how they can impact on the performance of coaches.

In order to come from an emotionally intelligent position, we need to have an 'I'm ok, you're ok' attitude. In other words, we need to value and respect ourselves for who we are, while at the same time valuing and respecting others for who they are, even if we disagree with their values, attitudes and actions.

I'm not ok You're ok Passive **The submissive coach:** subjective intentions about boosting coach's own self-regard	I'm ok You're ok Healthy Assertive **The EI coach:** successful, authentic, positive, objective intentions
I'm not ok You're not ok Stuck Passive-aggressive **The hopeless coach:** doubting success of coaching and possible benefits to client	I'm ok You're not ok Judgement Aggressive **The directive coach:** subjective intentions about manipulating client

Figure 3.2   The ok corral

The EI coach ('I'm ok, you're ok')

As we saw in Chapter 2, there is no universal agreement on what coaching is. Does a successful coach always have to be non-directive? Do coaches need to know more about the topic being discussed than the people they are coaching in order for the coaching to succeed?

Using the life positions as the foundation to successful coaching, we believe that the coach needs to have an 'I'm ok, you're ok' attitude for the coaching to be successful. Given this set of healthy attitudes, the coach's intention will always be to support the person being coached in the best way possible. While this support will essentially be in the form of skilled, non-directive questioning and listening, it may also involve slightly more directive ideas for developing attitudes, thoughts and behaviours.

The coach's attitudes and intentions are just as important as his/her coaching skills. From this foundation, we offer the following definition of the EI coach:

> The emotionally intelligent coach uses a combination of skills, healthy 'I'm ok, you're ok' attitudes, self- and other awareness and expertise to facilitate the growth and development of their coachees. Underlying this skilled facilitation is the positive intention to always strive to be coachee-focused, with the EI

coach authentically aiming to use his or her attitudes, awareness and skills to support the coachee in the best possible way.

So, the 'I'm ok, you're ok' position is where emotionally intelligent coaches sit – comfortable and confident with who they are, and positive about the impact their coaching will have. If you're in this position, you may:

- feel that your coaching is in the flow, it's authentic;
- have more work than you can cope with;
- see successful coachees through your business on a regular basis;
- believe in the ability of all coachees to make sustainable change;
- hold yourself and your coachees in unconditional positive regard.

The submissive coach (I'm not ok, you're ok)

Have you ever noticed how some people with low self-esteem are attracted to jobs where they surround themselves with people who apparently have more problems than they do? They then happily fill the role of helper, always going the extra mile to help others and pleased to receive the recognition for doing this along the way. Do you know 'helpers' who spend most of the time focusing on helping others, rarely stopping to look at what they need to develop about themselves?

If you're in this position, you may:

- collude with your coachee unintentionally by not challenging his or her negative self-talk and self-regard;
- agree with your coachee – bringing yourself and your opinions into the session inappropriately;
- coach for longer than the agreed session length because you're uncomfortable being assertive or drawing it to a close if the coachee is still talking;
- be over-accommodating when the coachee calls to change session times, or turns up late;
- be unwilling to address the challenge that coaching may not be the most appropriate intervention, as you don't want to upset your coachee;
- avoid challenging with powerful questions about goal setting, reality checks and beliefs;
- form an inappropriate attachment if your coachee seems to be what you aspire to be;
- become anxious about taking on new coachees;
- believe that it's your fault if your coachees don't make any progress towards their goals or return for more sessions;

Activity

What else might happen if you are a submissive coach? It's worth taking a moment to give this some thought – this will also help raise your self-awareness about your own practice.

The directive coach (I'm ok, you're not ok)

Directive coaches often come from a position of negative intention. For this type of coach, coaching is just a clever way of getting your coachee to do exactly what you want them to do, without the coachee being consciously aware of it. At worst, the directive coach simply views coaching as a sophisticated form of manipulation. The direction offered by a directive coach differs from direction offered by an EI coach. The difference is intention. Whilst a directive coach deliberately wants to manipulate the coachee without showing them regard, EI coaches will only offer direction when they feel it is genuinely in the best interests of the coachee, and then only with permission from their coachee.

I'm ok/you're not ok

As we know from Chapter 1, this position often masks the previous life position of I'm not ok/you're ok, and as a coach we need to be aware of this so that we can reflect honestly as to where we are.

If you're in this position, you may:

- ask more judgemental questions such as 'why'. This can sometimes be used effectively, but must absolutely come from an 'I'm ok, you're ok' position. We will discuss this more in the chapter on coaching skills;
- unconsciously use a more critical voice tone;
- unconsciously display more critical body language such as a frown or raised eyebrows;
- be inflexible when a coachee needs to rearrange the session;
- feel disapproval if your coachee doesn't hold the same values or beliefs as you do;
- feel that coaching doesn't work because most coachees are too needy or not ready to be coached;
- lose coachees, but believe it's all about them and their issues.

Activity

What else might happen if you are a directive coach?

The hopeless coach (I'm not ok, you're not ok)

Coaches with this set of attitudes do exist! These are coaches who doubt their own capacity to coach while at the same time doubting the benefits of coaching to their coachee.

If you're in this position, you may:

 give up coaching – it almost certainly will seem hard work and stressful;

- display some of the attitudes and characteristics of being in either the 'I'm ok, you're not ok' quadrant, or the 'I'm not ok, you're ok' quadrant;
- lose coachees;
- avoid taking on new coachees as you're not sure you could help them, even if you felt they were capable of being helped;
- alternate between being passive and aggressive in your relationship with your coachee;
- feel anxious, lacking in confidence or even show signs of depression about your career.

Activity

What else might happen if you are a hopeless coach?

Self-awareness

As we saw in Chapter 1, self-awareness is about being aware of your own feelings and learning how to manage them, rather than allowing them to manage you.

Coaches are human, and unfortunately there is not a button on the back of a coach's neck we can press that will switch off his or her attitudes, values and feelings before he or she starts a coaching session. It is therefore inevitable that coachees will say things that will trigger emotional responses in the coach from time to time, particularly if what the coachees say is closely connected to one of the coach's attitudes or values.

The self-aware coach will manage this process, both at the time and through reflective learning and supervision afterwards. This is an essential quality for a coach to have. As we saw in the coaching dialogue with Charlotte, allowing your own attitudes to seep into a coaching session will often lead to ineffective coaching. Let's have a look at how the coach, Charlotte, could have dealt with the situation better.

Coach (Charlotte): So what would you like to talk about today?

Coachee: One of the women on my team; she is proving difficult to work with.

Coach: What exactly is the problem?

Coachee: She never does what I ask her and this is putting extra pressure on me.

Coach: What do you think the reason is?

Coachee: I hate to say it, but I think it's because she's a woman.

Coach: What do you mean?

Coachee: Well, women are scattier than men and often promise things they can't deliver.

Coach: (pause) What can you do to improve this situation with her?

Coachee: (pause) I don't know, I suppose I could talk to her.

Coach: What could you say to her?

Coachee: I could tell her that I feel her behaviour is not reliable and that this bothers me.

Coach: What do you need to do to make this happen?

The difference here is there is no judgement being allowed to seep into the coach's behaviour. As the coachee does not feel judged (normally being judged will be picked up by our emotional brain), he is more willing to open up and look at the solution. Who knows, he may have even been deliberately trying to provoke his coach with the statement about women. By pausing and using a non-judgemental question, the coach has showed that she will not be drawn into a values conflict with her coachee.

Developing your self-awareness is a habit that we can all learn. This habit involves three simple steps:

1. Stop and notice the emotions you are feeling.
2. Give a name to these emotions.
3. Understand these emotions and manage them before they manage you.

The following example demonstrates how this simple three-step habit can be applied.

Morten the unhappy colleague

Claus was delighted. He had just had his annual performance review with his manager and had been told he was being offered a promotion, which meant he would be relocated to Southern France. Naturally, Claus was keen to share his good news, and the first person he saw when he came out of the review was his colleague Morten. On sharing the news, Claus was surprised by Morten's reaction. Rather than being pleased, Morten seemed annoyed by the news and reluctantly congratulated Claus on his reward. Claus was even more surprised to find that for the next few weeks, Morten seemed to avoid him. He even found out that Morten had been criticizing him to other colleagues, telling people how Claus was not a conscientious worker and took more breaks than the rest of the team.

So, what do you think was going on for Morten here? How could he have used his self-awareness to turn this situation into something more positive? Let's take the same story again, but this time with Morten using the three steps of self-awareness.

Morten the self-aware colleague

Claus was delighted. He had just had his annual performance review with his manager and had been told he was being offered a promotion, which meant he would be relocated to Southern France. Naturally, Claus was keen to share his good news, and the first person he saw when he came out of the review was his colleague Morten. On hearing the news, Morten was aware that he got an uncomfortable feeling inside his stomach. He congratulated Claus on his reward, but went away with these uneasy feelings. Morten stopped for a moment to ask himself what was going on. He realized that he was feeling irritated by the news because he was jealous. He wanted to be offered a promotion to Southern France and didn't feel it was fair that Claus got the reward. He was also feeling a little sad as Claus was a good friend, and life around the office would be pretty boring without him. Morten decided to arrange a meeting with his boss to explain that he would also like to progress in his career and to talk about what was needed to get a promotion. He also decided he would invite his new colleague Peter out for lunch and get to know him a little better. Having made these decisions, Morten noticed that the uncomfortable feeling in his stomach had gone.

How is our self-awareness linked to awareness of others? When we are interpreting how others are feeling and why, we use ourselves as the diagnostic tool. We will now move on to look at how we diagnose others and why it is important for any coach (and manager) to have a high awareness of others.

Awareness of others

Awareness of others is perhaps one of the most important skills a coach requires. In order to have high awareness of others, you need to be tuned in to their feeling states and be aware of how certain things are impacting on them. Building rapport and open communication is therefore essential, as is being able to listen on an intuitive level to your coachees.

Listen with your eyes and whole body, not just with your ears

Most research on communication agrees that the majority of the communication process is non-verbal. Eye contact, facial expression, tone and volume of voice and body language are far more likely to give you an idea about how a coachee is feeling than just listening to the words he or she says.

Amazingly, our brains are pre-programmed to pick up on these signals, feel the emotions of others and even mirror the behaviours of other people. Have you ever had someone smile at you and find yourself smiling too? Have you ever been to a presentation and noticed an uncomfortable feeling in your stomach because the presenter seems really nervous? This reaction will have been down to a set of nerve cells in our emotional brain (midbrain) that Daniel Goleman calls 'mirror neurones'. Goleman argues that, as we are social animals, we have these neurones to enable us to bond with and understand others. As an important part of any coaching relationship is building rapport and understanding your coachee, these mirror neurones are an essential part of a coach's toolbox.

However, these mirror neurones will only be helpful if we use them. If we do not develop our regard for others and develop relationships with an 'I'm ok, you're ok' attitude then these powerful, rapport-building tools will not be used.

Authentic rapport versus manipulating rapport

Have you ever been on a sales course where you are taught to manipulate your counterpart by consciously mirroring their behaviour in an attempt to get them to trust you? Unfortunately (or fortunately!) this type of mirroring is unlikely to have a positive effect at an emotional level. Our emotional brains are incredibly adept at picking up on authentic behaviour in others, and conscious attempts to manipulate will normally leave your counterpart feeling uneasy in some way. Manipulation stems from the emotionally unintelligent 'I'm ok, you're not ok' attitude. This attitude rarely if ever pays off.

Developing rapport from a balanced 'I'm ok, you're ok' attitude, on the other hand, will lead to increased trust, openness and cooperation. When true rapport is achieved, two people often unconsciously mirror each other's behaviour. Have you ever spent time in a cafe or restaurant observing two people who are close friends or in love? Next time you are out look out for this, paying careful attention to how body language and even dress sense are mirrored.

However, unlike a relationship between two friends, a coach needs to use to learn this deeper understanding and mirroring of others in a controlled way. Imagine if every time a coachee got angry or started crying, the coach did the same! So, for a coach, even though his or her mirror neurones will help him or her to 'feel' what the coachee is feeling and build rapport, the coach must also use his or her self-awareness to manage these feelings, not allowing them to impact on his or her own behaviour.

Warning: jumping to conclusions is dangerous

Being aware of when a coachee's tone changes when talking about certain topics, and being aware of a coachee's body language and facial expressions, are valuable to a coach. However, it can also be dangerous to assume you know how your coachee is feeling, as the following extract from a coach-coachee dialogue demonstrates:

Coach: So what can you do about improving this situation?

Coachee: (looking down and in a quiet voice) I'm not sure, I suppose I could talk to him.

Coach: You are obviously not motivated to do this. What can you do to change this?

Coachee: No, I do want to do it. It's just I'm not sure how to approach him.

Clearly the coach made a big error here, jumping to conclusions about how the coachee was feeling. Remember: you can never know how someone else is feeling unless he or she tells you!

Have you ever had someone tell you how you are feeling? Statements like, 'I know you are disappointed' or, 'I can tell you are angry' are judgements. Nobody likes to be judged or told how they are feeling. However, having a high awareness of others can help you to ask powerful questions connected to what you think the coachee may be feeling. Powerful questions the coach could have used in the above example are, 'I'm sensing something here – what might it be?' 'I noticed your voice became quieter and you looked down then? What is that telling you?'

Developing the core coaching competencies of building rapport, being empathic, asking good open questions and listening with your eyes will all help coaches to increase their awareness of others. We will look at these competencies in more depth in Chapter 7.

Empathy: the antidote to judgement

Empathy is about imagining what things might be like from another person's perspective. The following story provides a simple example of how easy it is to only see things from your own perspective.

Little Ben at the zoo

John and Sally took their 3-year old son, Ben, to the zoo. Ben particularly wanted to see the lions, so the first place they went to was the lion's den. John told Ben to look at the lions and asked him what he thought. Ben responded by looking unhappy, which frustrated his father who said, 'Go on Ben, do as you're told, look at the lions.' Sally realized that Ben was unable to see the lions properly because of the high wall, so went over to her son and picked him up. Immediately Ben began to smile and pointed to the lions.

How often do you see things only from your own perspective? As soon as you start judging people and fail to notice the emotions they are expressing, you stop hearing them and will fail to appreciate their perspective.

The EI coach (high awareness of self and others)

It is a myth that coaches should be 'empty vessels' when working with coachees, freeing themselves of any judgements and emotions to enable them to focus on their coachees in an entirely objective way. Coaches do not have an emotion and values on/off switch they can disengage before starting

Low self-awareness High awareness of others **The other-focused coach**	High self-awareness High awareness of others **The EI coach present, tuned in to self and others**
Low self-awareness Low awareness of others **The unaware coach**	High self-awareness Low awareness of others **The self-focused coach**

Figure 3.3   Awareness and types of coach

a coaching session. Coaches will experience real emotions and judgements, just like any other human being.

However, having high levels of self- and other awareness will allow coaches to minimize their own subjectivity, enabling them to remain predominantly coachee-focused, as Figure 3.3 indicates.

EI coaches will be tuned in to their own intuitions and feelings, using them to understand their coachees better while managing any strong emotions they feel themselves during coaching. At the same time, EI coaches will be aware of any emotional cues their coachee sends out, using these cues to improve their understanding of the coachee.

The other-focused coach (low self-awareness, high awareness of others)

Other-focused coaches will tend to focus excessively on the feeling states of others while paying little attention to their own intuitions and emotional hijacks. This may lead to ineffective coaching as such coaches are more likely to allow their own judgements and emotions to intervene in the coaching, without having the awareness to press their pause button and prevent them from leading the coachee in a directive way.

The self-focused coach (high self-awareness, low awareness of others)

Self-focused coaches are likely to stick to their own agenda rather than the coachee's. Without paying careful attention to their coachee's choice of words, body language cues, facial expressions and voice tone variations, this type of coach is likely to miss out on vital information.

The unaware coach (low self-awareness, low awareness of others)

Perhaps the most ineffective of all four awareness combinations, this coach is likely to view coaching as a rational activity, focusing on facts and actions, but overlooking emotional cues both in him- or herself and others. Coaching from an emotionally unaware position is like navigating without a map or a compass: it is likely to be ineffective, wasting lots of time, and is potentially dangerous!

A note about trust

As well as having highly developed life positions and awareness, successful coaches need to be trustworthy. This will stem from having a high regard for others. If you genuinely value your coachees and want them to benefit from the coaching, you are more likely to be trustworthy and reliable. Behaving in a trustworthy way is essential for a coach. This includes helping the coachee to set realistic expectations of coaching at the outset. If, in trying to sell your coaching, you make unrealistic claims and later the coachee finds that these claims are not substantiated, he or she will inevitably lose trust in you and, potentially, the coaching profession. Also, it is important to keep your promises. Imagine the impact of a coach telling his or her coachee that he or she would write up the notes and e-mail them later that day. When it doesn't happen, or takes a few days, the coachee may feel less inclined to view the coach as trustworthy and reliable.

Acting in a trustworthy way is also contagious. If you keep your word and do exactly as you say you will do, your coachees are more likely to do the same. So, for example, if they say they will report back to you on their actions at the end of the week, there is a better chance of them doing this, rather than thinking, 'Well, he said he'd send me my notes but he didn't, so he can't really moan if I'm a few days late with my e-mail.'

Inviting the trust of others and self-regard

Often, when someone lacks trustworthiness, it may not be a deliberate attempt to manipulate and deceive others.

A change of opinion?

George knew his work colleague Tom was a big football fan. When Tom asked him if he liked football, he answered with enthusiasm, telling Tom how much he loved the game. At the same time, he knew his other colleague Julian hated football. In fact, he regularly heard Julian expressing his dislike of football and commenting on how boring he found Tom's obsession with the game. When alone with Julian, George often found himself agreeing with Julian, even to the extent where he would criticize Tom and his childish obsession with 'grown men chasing a ball'.

The inconsistent behaviour shown by George does not invite the trust of others. Why do you think George behaves the way he does? Could it be that he has a conditional self-regard of 'I'm ok as long as others like me'? Could it be that as a result, George avoids conflict and has developed a habit of agreeing with others?

Summary

- Allowing emotionally unintelligent coaches to coach can be ineffective and costly.
- An EI coach has highly developed regard for self and others, high levels of self- and other-awareness, combined with the required skills and knowledge to be an effective coach.
- 'I'm ok as long as I help others' and 'I'm ok as long as I control others' are common attitudes that lead to ineffective coaching and management.
- Having a high regard for others will mean than a coach's intentions are coachee-focused and positive.
- Unconscious, and therefore authentic, mirroring and rapport between the coach and the coachee will stem from high regard for others.
- Self-awareness is essential to prevent coaches from allowing their own values, attitudes and emotions to make subjective judgements of their coaches.
- Having high awareness of others will provide a coach with essential emotional cues.
- Inviting trust is essential when building an open, effective coaching relationship.

References

Goleman, D (2006) *Social Intelligence,* Hutchinson, London

Harris, T (1995) *I'm OK, You're OK,* Arrow Books, London

Sparrow, T and Knight, A (2006) *Applied EI,* Wiley, Chichester

4

The fast track to performance and profitability

> *The achievements of an organization are the results of the combined effort of each individual.*
>
> Vincent Lombardi

Imagine a team of 11 players about to play in a cup final game, the pinnacle of their career and the team's season. They're lined up in the tunnel about to go on to the pitch, they can hear their fans singing and the energy is electric. Three of the team are feeling really anxious and their self-talk is on overdrive. 'What are you doing here, you'll never score, winning cup finals happens to other people' are just some of the attitudes that are showing up in their thinking and in the churning of their stomachs. Now fast forward to the end of the game; do you think this team has won? How will this team, with some of the players having negative attitudes, have performed? No surprises when we tell you they lost and at what cost? This will cost the team in terms of confidence, pride and also in the tangible costs of sales of merchandise, season tickets, share price, etc. Will this affect profitability? You bet it will. Would you invest your money in such a team? What could they have done differently? To start with their coach (their leader) could have been more tuned into how these players were feeling and coached them to manage their emotions and attitudes to best effect. The individuals could have taken responsibility for themselves and either asked for support or worked through the emotions and managed them differently, though this isn't something we're taught how to do generally in life.

Now consider this happening in an organization, where some of the employees have negative attitudes. Will this really affect the performance and profitability of the organization? Let's consider that each employee has 100 per cent potential, whatever that means to them, and yet they're possibly just dipping into 35 to 40 per cent of their treasure chest of resources. How do you think they'll be performing as individuals and how will this affect the team performance? With negative attitudes afoot there will be an impact on productivity and performance at all levels. If this is rife across an organization, there will undoubtedly be repercussions on profit levels and share prices. Negativity does cost!

PAYING THE PRICE OF NEGATIVITY

The US Bureau of Labor Statistics did some research and estimated that negative beliefs and attitudes in the workplace cost US industry approximately $3 billion per year (Buzzan, 2001). Think about that for a moment: where did that cost come from? Undoubtedly the bottom line of many organizations.

Therefore, ignore the attitude element at your peril! What are negative attitudes costing you personally and the organization you're part of/leading? Gary Topchik, of the American Management Association, when asked about this figure said, 'besides making the office an unhappy place to work, workplace negativity affects the bottom line: it affects productivity and profit margins; turnover increases; absenteeism increases; customer complaints increase. It becomes a huge business issue' (Buzzan, 2001). It's official: negative attitudes are contagious and they cost in terms of performance and bottom line!

The price of poor leadership

A team of sales consultants who work for a financial services company and have been working together for two years, are told that they are being bought out by a high street bank. Immediately the team's emotional response is to be anxious, think about whether they'll still have a job, wonder who'll be their new leaders and what they'll be like. It undoubtedly means changes for the team, and when the new Director and his team take over, they're called into a meeting, told their jobs are all safe, and initially feel relieved. Then they're told they need to talk to their clients about the changes and are staggered to know they're expected to tell them something that is blatantly not true. Imagine how they're feeling – concerned, confused about the mixed messages and their own credibility, angry and frustrated – to name a few emotions.

The team approached the Director and talked about their concerns. The response knocked them even more when they were informed that this wasn't negotiable (if you don't like it you know where the door is). How productive do you think this team was over the coming days and weeks? Not very, with the main topic of conversation being the disbelief at the approach of this large, supposedly professional organization. The Director picked up on this and held a meeting with the team to inform them that they needed to start performing or they'd be disciplined. Within a few weeks a process of performance management started, with one of the team receiving a letter inviting him to a formal meeting with his manager and HR manager. The impact? Demotivated staff, negative feelings towards the Director and the organization, a general attitude of 'what's the point' and a dip in the sales figures. Within 12 months of the changes, the whole team had left the organization.

The EI coaching difference

So what difference could emotional intelligence coaching have made? With the support of EI coaching the individual sales consultants would have recognized what was going on with their feelings and the impact of these feelings. They would have known what they wanted to do with them and they would have made their end decisions quicker (either to get out of the organization or make a strong stand to the CEO of the organization). They would have identified a productive, healthy, way forward more quickly.

In terms of the six main areas of EI we introduced in Chapter 1, which of them impacted on the performance of the sales consultants and in what ways? First of all there was a definite lack of regard for others, both for the sales consultants team and for the clients who the Director was expecting the team to string along. There seemed to be no awareness of others; despite the fact the team expressed their concerns, the new management team didn't care. In terms of self-awareness this was different for each team member; two of them had definite 'emotional hijacks', which caused them to behave in erratic, almost self-destructive ways that just weren't their normal behaviours. With greater self-awareness they would have recognized the emotions and pressed the pause button. When the leadership team started down the performance management route, this unsurprisingly affected the self-regard of some of the team, who valued themselves based on what they achieved (a conditional self-regard of 'I'm ok as long as I achieve my targets at work').

From the examples so far, you will see that attitudes are highly important in the performance equation and can become a large part of the interferences (if negative) or contribute towards the potential being really tapped into (if positive). As we've already mentioned, attitudes are a key element of EI. EI coaching has an important role to play in individual, team and organization performance, so let's look at each individually.

THE POTENTIAL AND PERFORMANCE EQUATION

As discussed in Chapter 1, the potential equation highlights how we could improve performance, and we'd like to expand that some more here. As Tim Gallwey said, 'In every human endeavour there are two arenas of engagement: the outer and the inner.'

The outer arena is what we see happening externally. For example, for a sales person it could be the results he or she is achieving (or not, as the case may be) and the inner arena is about the internal attitudes and values either supporting that achievement or getting in their way. This is about overcoming our own obstacles, such as self-doubt, over-analysing situations, fear, assumptions we're making, and limiting beliefs.

So let's review that equation once again:

$$P = p - i \text{ (Performance = potential - interferences)}$$

The way to increase performance, using this equation, is to grow and develop the 'p' factor, the potential, and to reduce or eliminate the 'i' interferences.

The great training robbery! Why training sometimes doesn't work

In Chapter 1 we introduced the KASH model (Knowledge, Attitudes, Skills, Habits) and its importance in all development. The spend on training globally is huge and yet the sad thing is that a lot of it doesn't work. It is being increasingly recognized that the way organizations can stand out from their competitors is through their people. We often hear the mantra, 'Our people are our best asset' and yet too few organizations actually do anything about it.

Consider the work done by Detterman and Sternberg (1993) on the transfer of learning. Their research suggests that the useful transfer of training back to work may be as low as 10 per cent (from US evidence). Just think about the billions of dollars a year that could be being wasted taking people out of work, sharing new information, ideas and skills that are never actually used!

We believe the KASH model is the key to determining 'the quality of human performance in any given situation or context'. When you talk to organizations and ask them which elements of the KASH model they tend to use in their training programmes, the answer is nearly always 'knowledge and skills'.

Henry and the training disaster

Henry, the Training and Development Manager of a large manufacturing company, had recognized there was a need for their new graduates to do a presentation skills course. He arranged for a training company to come in and deliver its programme to the team. The trainers, Presenting Specialists Ltd, had a good reputation and delivered its standard courses as open courses and in companies. Henry e-mailed the graduates to let them know they'd be on a one-day training course the following month and to put time aside in their diaries.

When the trainer from Presenting Specialists turned up on the morning of the training, he was met by 12 people who were not sure why they had been sent and certainly gave the impression they didn't want to be there. So the trainer, Lesley, spent the first hour talking about the course and almost trying to sell it to the participants. The graduates went through the motions of listening and doing group and individual exercises, and overall the day went quite well.

Henry was pleased that he'd identified and solved an important training need, though this was soon questioned when some of the team were asked to do presentations at the next company meeting. Some of the presentations were awful, not enough preparation had been done, some people were reading off their PowerPoint slides, some of them simply weren't engaging. Henry's heart sank as he watched them in action. What had gone wrong? He simply coudn't understand it.

So, what went wrong? Henry had identified the area for development in the team and taken quite a simplistic, mechanistic view that a one-day standard presentation skills course would solve it (introducing purely knowledge and skills). Why did he do that? He had the best of intentions, but this was his standard approach and what he always did, ie a habit. What he hadn't taken into account was the need to inform those involved about why they were going on the training and what it would entail, or the attitudes of the individuals going on the training. He also didn't ask the trainer to tailor the programme or include attitudes and habits to really embed new behaviours. They didn't look at how people felt about making presentations or what their interferences might be, or give ideas about how to address this. This would have required skilled facilitation rather than straightforward training or instruction.

INDIVIDUAL PERFORMANCE

To be the very best version of you and perform at the peak of your potential, consider the EI model we talked about in Chapter 1. How do you rate yourself out of 10 on the six core areas (1 being very low, 10 being very high):

Self-regard   _____
Regard for others   _____
Self-awareness   _____
Awareness of others   _____
Self-management   _____
Relationship management   _____

In Chapter 5 there is a questionnaire for you to assess yourself on the first four areas of emotional intelligence. These undoubtedly impact on your performance. In fact, if we were to ask you to consider what percentage of your personal potential you are using in your life right now, what would you say? If you've said lower than 100 per cent (and by the way we've never met anyone so far who says he or she is using 100 per cent of their potential in all areas of their life), then your performance is going to be lower than it could be. Sir John Whitmore did some research into how much potential is used in the workplace, by simply asking people, 'How much of your potential do you use at work?' The overall average came out at around 40 per cent! Think about that for a moment: if you are using just 40 per cent of your potential, what is happening to the other 60 per cent?

Activity: Your current role and the KASH model

Think about your current role and how you feel about it. What is your performance really like? How would you rate your knowledge? Is it enough for you to be high performing? What about your attitudes? Are they more positive or negative towards your job and the organization itself? What about your skill levels: do they meet the requirements of your job? What are the habits, daily behaviours that you see in yourself? Do they really support you to be as successful as possible? Which of these areas, if any, would you like to develop? Rate yourself out of 10 in each of these areas, 1 being low in knowledge and skills and more negative attitudes and habits, 10 being couldn't be better/more positive.

Knowledge	Attitudes
Skills	Habits

Figure 4.1   The KASH quadrant

Then complete the boxes with elements you'd like to develop in terms of knowledge, attitudes, skills and habits, so as to improve your performance.

TEAM PERFORMANCE

The P = p - i formula works just as well at the individual level as it does at macro levels within a team, department or whole organization. Imagine that you have a team working together and each individual brings his or her 'p' (potential) factor as well as his or her own 'i' internal interferences. On the one hand the internal interferences when brought together can mean they multiply and ultimately reduce the effectiveness of the team as a whole; on the other, the huge potential everyone brings can make a massive positive difference to team productivity and performance.

Gemma and the interference virus

Gemma hears on the office grapevine that the company figures aren't as good as expected and there'll be some changes coming. She doesn't clarify what that means or ask her boss; instead she tells her colleague Geoff at the photocopier that she thinks there's going to be some redundancies. Geoff has a few financial problems at home and starts to worry about being made redundant – how will he and his family manage? He tells Sharon in the marketing team about the forthcoming redundancies and back at her desk she tells her colleague Gareth. Gareth hasn't been with the company that long and he starts thinking about 'last in first out' and how this always happens to him and decides to go out at lunchtime to get the jobs' paper as he'd better starting looking around. Throughout the day and the rest of the week they tell other colleagues. This has a different impact for each of them according to their attitudes and values.

While the negative attitudes kick in, guess what happens to the team's focus, concentration, productivity and ultimately their performance that week? Undoubtedly it will drop.

What could they have done differently with awareness and emotional intelligence? First of all, Gemma could have checked with her boss about what was happening and what changes there could be, instead of adding 2 and 2 and making 10. Negative attitudes are contagious! Something happens in the company; someone isn't happy and doesn't have the confidence or inclination to talk to the boss; they tell their colleagues; it spreads and detracts from how people are working and their effectiveness.

Activity

Think of a time when you worked within an ineffective team. When you think back and reflect, what interferences were going on, for yourself and possibly others?

If we look at this from the alternative perspective – when a team is working together and brings their potential to the table with a minimum of interference going on – then the team's potential multiplies. The whole is definitely greater than the sum of its parts.

Activity

Think of a time when you worked within a high performing team. What was going on that made that team work well together?

The team effectiveness measurement tool (Maddocks and Sparrow, 2000) is a great way to look at what is really going on with respect to the team's levels of emotional intelligence. Sparrow and Knight in their book *Applied EI* (2006) liken it to an endoscopy, which really gets down to what is going on. The tool deals with seven core aspects of team behaviours:

1. motivation and commitment;
2. conflict handling;
3. team climate;
4. self-management;
5. relationship management;
6. openness of communication;
7. tolerance of differences.

Activity: Your team and their performance

Consider how you would rate your team in these seven areas. If there were one area for improvement what would it be? How could you begin to address this? Use Table 4.1 to generate ideas.

Table 4.1 Your team's performance

Team Behaviour	Rating 1–10	Actions
1. Motivation and Commitment		
2. Conflict Handling		
3. Team Climate		
4. Self-management		
5. Relationship Management		
6. Openness of Communication		
7. Tolerance of Differences		

EI team development and coaching in action

We interviewed Saulius Sabunas, General Manager of AstraZeneca, Lithuania, about some team EI and coaching development he'd undertaken with us. This was what he had to say about it.

AstraZeneca

I started with AstraZeneca at the beginning of 2000 and the company was very successful, one of the best companies in Lithuania at that time. After five years we ended up in a difficult situation as the company was not growing as it had been. I had major health problems and was in hospital and off work for more than a month. The results for an 18-month period weren't so good, our growth was lower than the industry growth, there were disagreements between people, the spirit was lost, and meetings were very challenging.

We had the team EI development programme, including 360-degree feedback, which was very challenging, as was the seminar. There were lots of interpersonal issues between the management team and there was lots of blaming. This programme enabled us to express these feelings, get them all out on the table. After two days on the programme, I'd told my team everything, both positive and negative. We had a full inventory of feelings from everyone. Then, we started to talk to move forward, to create rules how we can work together.

The situation at work became very different as a result of what we'd learnt. We started asking, 'How do you feel?' at the beginning of meetings and checking out at the end with, 'How do you feel that went?' We used (and still do) the practice of praising people publicly; using chairmanship rotation, we communicate minutes of meetings immediately. We produced a small booklet about leadership, how to give feedback, about the coaching model TGROW, etc.

The combination of EI and team coaching facilitated some really positive sustainable changes and this had a huge impact on performance and people's own personal health and wellbeing, as well as a sense of satisfaction.

I believe there is a very strong relationship between EI, coaching and performance. My advice to other top leaders about how to get strong, successful relationships with your team would be that while it is very important to recognize the importance of tasks/objectives, it's also essential to recognize that people's feelings are very important. Now when I'm employing people, competencies are not the most important factor (you can train them); values and emotional intelligence factors are hugely important.

Having good coaching combined with EI is important for successful performance. I believe my job is not about advising and giving all the solutions. My job is asking questions to help my team to find their solutions. When our company was rated this year it was judged to be one of the top performing companies in this region, partly because of its image and our positive attitude.

Saulius is a great example of an emotionally intelligent leader who uses a coaching style to improve performance.

ORGANIZATIONAL PERFORMANCE

Recent Gallup research shows some interesting results (see www.gmj.gallup.com). Organizations with high engagement are:

- 50 per cent more likely to have lower staff turnover;
- 56 per cent more likely to have higher than average customer loyalty;
- 38 per cent more likely to have above average productivity;
- 27 per cent more likely to report above average profitability.

Sears, a US company, found that every 5 per cent increase in employee satisfaction leads to a 1.3 per cent improved customer impression, which in turn drives a 0.5 per cent in profit growth. What did this mean? The difference of $200 million a year! An engaged workforce has trust and openness, builds effective relationships inside and outside the organization, which ultimately makes a difference to the bottom line. These are all elements of the organization's EI.

THE EVIDENCE

EI and the performance link

Remember the study we mentioned in Chapter 1 carried out by The Carnegie Institute that concluded that 85 per cent of financial success comes from human engineering and only approximately 15 per cent comes from technical skills and abilities? Success is not all about the qualifications and technical elements of performance. Indeed, it's more about the EI elements (how well you value yourself, how you value others, how well tuned in you are to other people and yourself, plus how you interact with others and how you manage yourself).

The amount of research linking EI and performance at work is growing, and we'll highlight some of the key evidence for you here. We have used two core resources for this: 'The business case for emotional intelligence', a paper written by Cary Cherniss, of Rutgers University for the Consortium for Research on Emotional Intelligence in Organizations (see www.eiconsortium.com), and *Linking Emotional Intelligence and Performance at Work* (Druskat *et al*, 2006).

Cherniss presents 19 different cases to illustrate how emotional intelligence contributes to the bottom line in any organization. For example, after supervisors in a manufacturing plant received training in EI, lost-time accidents were reduced by 50 per cent, formal grievances were reduced from an average of 15 to three per year, and the plant exceeded productivity goals by $250,000 (Pesuric and Byham, 1996).

Two pieces of research in the military, one in the US Air Force (USAF) and the other in the Israeli Defense Forces (IDF) (see Druskat *et al*, 2006*)*, examined the impact of EI on performance to see if it could be applied in recruiting the right people for the job and reducing mismatches. The IDF research was an in-depth study of more than 5,000 participants over a three-year period. Both pieces of research found overwhelmingly that there is a significant relationship between EI and occupational performance. They also found that EI can predict leadership potential. By using the EI model they'd worked with for the research, the USAF increased its ability to predict successful recruiters by nearly threefold, reduced the turnover of first-year recruits due to mismatches dramatically and cut its financial losses by approximately 92 per cent.

These are just a very small sample of the evidence for emotional intelligence and the link to performance and ultimately profitability.

Coaching and performance

The main coaching bodies (such as the International Coach Federation, European Mentoring and Coaching Council, Association of Coaching, etc), and other professional bodies such as CIPD (Chartered Institute of Personnel and Development) are contributing greatly towards the amount of research that is going on around linking coaching and performance.

In *The Case for Coaching*, Jarvis *et al* (2006) have trawled all the research on coaching and found that the vast majority of people they interviewed firmly believe that coaching creates improvements in the performance of individuals (96 per cent), which ultimately translates into results for the organizations they work for (87 per cent).

Michigan-based Triad Performance Technologies, Inc studied and evaluated the effects of coaching on a group of sales managers in a large telecoms organization. The research reports a 10:1 return on investment in less than one year. The study found that the following business outcomes were directly attributable to the coaching intervention:

- top performing staff who were considering leaving, were retained;
- reduced turnover of staff;
- increased revenue;
- improved customer satisfaction;

- a positive work environment was created, focusing on strategic account development and higher sales volume;
- revenues were increased, due to managers improving their performance and exceeding their goals.

A research paper (McGovern *et al*, 2001) reports a study of 100 executives in the United States. In the paper they show a model of establishing ROI and found that there were average returns of 5.7 times the initial investment in coaching, and tangible benefits such as 53 per cent of respondents reporting increases in productivity.

So what difference can EI coaching make?

Two of the key principles underlying EI are: 1) EI predicts performance, and 2) EI is changeable and can be developed.

Skilful coaching is the ideal way to build the EI of individuals, teams and indeed an entire organization. An EI coach can make the real difference here, though changing attitudes and habits is not necessarily a quick process. EI coaching does promise long-term change and sustainability, providing the conditions are right (as discussed in Chapter 3).

Ten situations where EI coaching could make a difference to performance

1. *Performance review and appraisals* – by using an EI coaching approach to performance reviews, both managers and team members could benefit.
2. *Improve sales* – as the case study of the Commercial and Fleet Manager at the car dealership in Chapter 2 shows, coaching can make a big difference to sales performance. Rather than the old fashioned view of sales people making the sale at any cost, an emotionally intelligent sales person (I'm ok, you're ok) will use a coaching style to establish the client's needs and make the appropriate suggestions. EI coaching is the foundation of a true win-win relationship.
3. *Change process* – the reason that many change processes don't work is poor communication. Emotionally intelligent leaders need to communicate the required changes clearly, and using a coaching approach to involve the various functions to implement the changes could make a huge difference.
4. *Mergers and acquisitions* – as with our case study earlier in this chapter, we saw the cost of a poor merger process.
5. *Redundancy* – being made redundant is a huge event in people's lives and how it's handled can make a big difference.

6. *Motivation* – have you ever worked in an organization where people do their jobs and get by with little enthusiasm or motivation, just getting through the day? What impact does this have on performance? A huge one! EI coaching can help individuals and managers understand what really motivates them.

7. *Creativity* – coaching an emotionally intelligent team who are looking to develop creative ideas for marketing their products or services, would see the 'p' potential factor being increased and therefore the performance increasing exponentially.

8. *Downturn in the economy* – when a downturn is predicted or starts to kick in, then it is easy for fear and negativity to set in. With the powerful combination of EI (including resilience and flexibility) and coaching, organizations can use the huge wealth of potential within their workforce to develop creative approaches to adapting.

9. *Recruitment and retention of staff* – the challenge for organizations is to attract talented staff to work for them and then to keep them. Coaching is a great way to develop these people and demonstrate they are valued and recognized.

10. *Overall leadership style* – Daniel Goleman in his book *Primal Leadership* (2002) talks about the six different styles of leadership and how a coaching style is a prerequisite of great leadership (we'll come to this later).

The following case study brings some of these situations to life. One of our clients, Statoil, achieved improved sales, a successful (and ongoing) change process, a more motivated workforce and a different productive style of leadership.

The emotionally intelligent leader

Morten Christensen, General Manager of Statoil, Lithuania

In July 2005, Morten took over the role of Operations Director and was responsible for the network of service stations. From November that year he became the new General Manager. The company was experiencing poor results and in fact negative results at the end of 2005, and yet Morten saw huge potential to improve many basic things. When he became General Manager the first thing he did was hold 20-minute one-to-one meetings with all the staff. This is what he said about it.

At the meetings I asked them questions like 'What are you doing? What are your tasks? What do you do when you're not at Statoil?' I made notes about each of them and referred back to them in conversation, which showed the staff, 'He's interested.'

Things started changing and we started earning money; attitudes and behaviour have shifted hugely. People are doing their jobs in a slightly different way. There's still a way to go and huge potential.

The main changes that have happened include 1) talking *to* people, not *about* people, rewarding and recognizing them for what they do; 2) informing them – they didn't know the company results and had never been told what was happening. Every month we hold breakfast meetings and we go through the financial results, what projects we're working on; everyone is involved in the company.

The level of openness increased and people started to trust the management team, as we involved them in the decisions.

The result? Our profit levels in 2005 were 0, in 2006 they were 7 million euros, and in 2007 they increased to 14 million euros!

Morten describes the leadership style as being an open, fair one that allows mistakes as long as people learn from them. The company has gone through a 360-degree feedback process and EI development programme, and there has been some great feedback, particularly about the levels of trust. The style has changed and has started to become more coaching and involving of others.

What can we learn from this case study? This is a great example of an organization that has an emotionally intelligent leader who resides in the healthy life position box of 'I'm ok, you're ok' and who values the people around him. He understands that to get the best out of people you have to really listen and get to know what motivates them. He used an open coaching style to start this whole process and the results on the bottom line have been dramatic.

Daniel Goleman talks about six different leadership styles and the importance of leaders having the flexibility to use all styles as and when appropriate. The six styles are coercive(directive), authoritarian (visionary), pace setting, coaching, democratic and affiliative. Morten operates across the spectrum of these styles as we saw in the case study. First of all he spent time considering the organization's position and met the team to get to know them (affiliative); he then held one-to-one meetings with the employees to really understand what motivated them (affiliative and coaching). Morten then spent time with the senior team to understand their position and points of view and asked what needed to be done(democratic), and went on to set the strategy in line with the vision and communicate this to the organization (authoritarian or visionary). Morten understands the potential that is within his organization and has an open door policy that encourages listening and challenging the status quo (coaching).

MEASURING THE IMPACT: WHAT'S YOUR ROI?

The use of coaching in organizations is on the rise across all sectors, including government departments, financial services, pharmaceutical companies and beyond. As coaching develops there's a higher demand for evaluation, measurement, and return on investment. While most people agree that measuring any people development initiatives is important, many feel that it's easier said than done. We believe a lot of coaching is not measured accurately, often because of the resources that organizations feel they'd need to commit to it.

In *The Case for Coaching* (Jarvis *et al*, 2006) there is a designated chapter on evaluation and a list of the benefits of evaluating coaching, including:

- It allows you to justify the investment in coaching in your organization.
- It allows you to benchmark your activities with other organizations.
- It can help to build support for coaching within the organization if positive results are seen.

What is important is to consider first of all why you want to measure the impact of coaching. Secondly, successful measurement will come about if and when evaluation is planned as early as possible, ie before the coaching starts. So just how do you measure the impact of coaching? You could use:

- employee attitude/climate surveys;
- staff turnover rates or improved retention of key staff;
- achievement of objectives set at the start of the coaching;
- comparison of pre/post-coaching 360-degree feedback ratings;
- improved appraisal/performance ratings.

The CIPD recommends the following six stages to measure the return on investment (ROI):

1. Verify changes in behaviour and results through discussion with the client.
2. Estimate the financial benefit of these changes.
3. Judge the role of coaching in enabling the changes.
4. Estimate the total financial benefit attributable to coaching.
5. Estimate the cost of providing coaching.
6. Calculate the return, ie the benefit relative to the cost.

Unfortunately, it's not common for organizations to carry out a full ROI on their coaching activities. Here's a case study of an organization, Skandia, that did measure the ROI of both emotional intelligence and coaching.

Skandia

Carla Ginn, Senior Learning and Development Adviser of Skandia spoke at the UK National EI Conference in 2006 about an emotional intelligence and coaching development programme some of Skandia's leaders went on. The key objectives of the programme were to improve the productivity and performance of their middle managers. The format of their programme is shown in Table 4.2.

Table 4.2 Skandia programme format

Knowledge	How	When
Introduction day	First meeting of group Including pre-work eg 'ie' profile	
Residential week	EI outdoor experiential learning and 'ie' profile debriefs	1 month after intro day
Follow-up day	Consolidate and revisit learning	1 month after residential
Three coaching sessions	For each participant of up to 1 hour	Monthly
Evaluation	Close out reports – evaluation of personal learning	After 8–12 weeks
	Questionnaires – participants and line managers	After the 3 coaching sessions

From the project and the measurements it carried out, Skandia found significant improvements in performance. It was able to measure the improvements and calculate the return on investment. Working out the ROI is an element that is commonly missed out, and with both EI and coaching it is entirely possible to do the calculation if you are willing to dedicate the appropriate resources to it.

There were 20 to 32 per cent performance improvements across the group, which showed the company got 20 to 32 per cent more out of the salary investment of the group of managers who received the development. The impact of EI development meant changes such as:

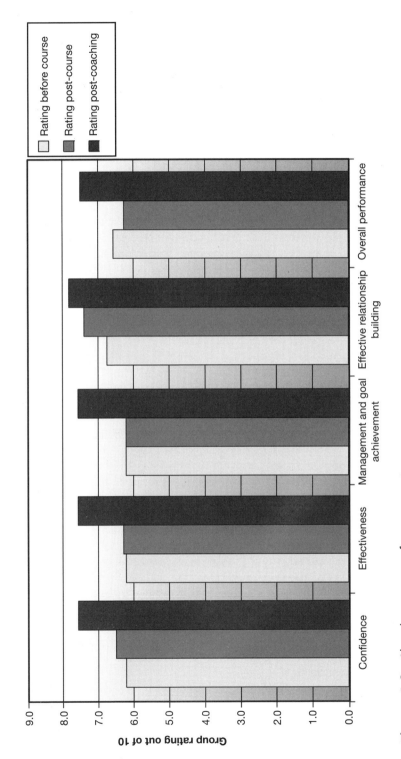

Figure 4.2 Skandia group performance ratings

- getting things right first time through self-belief;
- getting relationships right when it matters most;
- getting teams to deliver;
- tackling people issues;
- saving the company money from effective negotiations.

It calculated the return on investment using the formula:

$$ROI = \frac{Gross\ Benefit/Value - Cost}{Cost} \times 100\%$$

Its ROI worked out at £77,000 for the initial group of managers trained, which translated into 197 per cent (using external coaches) or 319 per cent (using internal coaches) of the cost of the programme (excluding time spent training). It identified some of the group performance ratings before and after the programme and after the coaching, shown in Figure 4.2, demonstrating what a positive impact the emotional intelligence development and coaching had.

Summary

- There is a clear link between emotionally intelligent coaching, performance and profitability.
- Research shows that EI and performance are linked.
- Research shows that coaching can have a positive impact on individual, team and organizational performance.
- Negative attitudes cost!
- Training works, as long as it addresses all the elements in the KASH model – Knowledge, Attitudes, Skills and Habits.
- You can improve organizational performance by decreasing the interferences that people have or increasing the potential they tap into. EI coaching is an ideal way to do this.
- EI coaching is a great way of enabling team development and performance, as shown in the case study of AstraZeneca.
- An emotionally intelligent leader uses coaching as one of his or her leadership styles to ensure high performance.
- EI coaching can change your life!
- EI coaching can support a wide range of organizational changes, developments, and strategy – see the section on 10 situations where EI coaching can make a difference.
- It is possible to measure the impact of EI coaching, as shown in the Skandia case study.

References

Buzzan, T (2001) *Head Strong*, Thorsons, London

CIPD (2004) *Buying Coaching Services*, CIPD, London

Detterman, D K and Sternberg, R J (1993) *Transfer on Trial: Intelligence, cognition and instruction*, Ablex, Norwood, NJ

Druskat, V U, Sala, F and Mount, G (2006) *Linking Emotional Intelligence and Performance at Work*, Lawrence Erlbaum, Philadelphia, PA

Goleman, D (2002) *Primal Leadership*, Harvard Business Press, Boston, MA

ICF (2001) *The Effectiveness of Coaching*, Results from international research, ICF, Lexington, KY

Jarvis, J, Land, D and Fillery-Travis, A (2006) *The Case for Coaching*, CIPD, London

McGovern, J, Lindemann, M, Vergara, M, Murphy, S, Barker, L and Warrenfeltz, R (2001) *The Manchester Review*, **6** (1)

Maddocks, J and Sparrow, T (2000) *The Team Effectiveness Questionnaire*, JCA Occupational Psychologists, Cheltenham

Pesuric, A and Byham, W (1996) The new look in behavior modeling, training and development, *Psychological Science*, **9** (5), pp 331–9

Sparrow, T and Knight, A (2006) *Applied EI*, Wiley, Chichester

5

Developing your emotional intelligence

> *A journey of a thousand miles begins with a single step.*
>
> Chinese proverb

> *Attitudes are nothing more than habits of thoughts, and habits can be acquired. An action repeated becomes an attitude realized.*
>
> Paul Myer

Who is the person you speak to most in your life? Your mother? Your brother? Your best friend? Your wife or husband?

The answer to this question is, of course, *yourself.* The whole time your conscious mind is awake, you are having a dialogue with yourself, telling yourself things and feeding information to your unconscious brain. This inner voice or inner coach is a powerful tool in helping you to develop your own emotional intelligence. Throughout this chapter, we will focus on using your inner coach to develop your own life positions and awareness.

In Chapter 3 we looked at the core elements needed for a coach (or anyone who isn't a coach!) to be emotionally intelligent. These are:

- high self-regard;
- high regard for others;
- high self-awareness;
- high awareness of others.

In this chapter, we provide concrete activities for developing your EI in relation to the above scales. To get the most from this section, you need to select and engage with the activities. To help you decide where to start focusing your attention, the following questionnaires will give you an approximate idea of which of the scales you might want to start with. As well as completing the questionnaires yourself, you may find it useful to ask a friend or colleague (someone who knows you quite well) to complete the questionnaires about you, so you can compare his or her responses to your own. You simply need to tell them to replace the 'I' in the questions with your name. When doing the questionnaires (which should only take about five minutes), try to answer honestly and quickly, without thinking about the responses too much. Avoid answering what you think you should answer; the more honest you are with yourself the better. Remember, as we discussed in Chapter 1, all aspects of EI can be changed, so a low score just gives you more opportunity to develop yourself in this area.

Part 1: Self-regard

Questions	5 ☺☺	4 ☺	3 Average	2 ☹	1 ☹☹
I regularly think positive thoughts about myself					
I tend to be optimistic					
I am comfortable saying 'no' to people and giving an honest explanation					
I take time to 'take in' and reflect on positive feedback other people give me					
I rarely, if ever, look to blame others					
I do not avoid conflict, but embrace it with assertive, positive behaviour					
I rarely, if ever, criticize my physical appearance					
I rarely, if ever, wish I was someone else					

Total score (out of 40) _____

Figure 5.1   Self-regard questionnaire

Part 2: Regard for others

Questions	5 ☺☺	4 ☺	3 Average	2 ☹	1 ☹☹
I regularly think positive thoughts about others					
I rarely, if ever, criticize other people for who they are – instead I focus on criticizing their behaviour					
I reject idle gossip about people in the news, reminding myself and others that I do not know the person					
I regularly give praise to others, both for their qualities as a person and actions					
I rarely, if ever, judge other people and brand them as 'good' or 'bad' people					
When disagreeing with another person, I focus on criticizing their actions and opinions, not who they are as a person					
I rarely, if ever, criticize the physical appearance of others					
I tend to focus on the strengths of others rather than their weaknesses					

Total score (out of 40) _____

Figure 5.2   Regard for others questionnaire

Part 3: Self-awareness

Questions	5 ☺☺	4 ☺	3 Average	2 ☹	1 ☹☹
I regularly pay attention to how I am feeling					
I am good at 'listening' to my body, reflecting on why I get pains, tension and other negative physical symptoms					
I believe emotions are at least as important as rational thoughts					
I am aware of how my body communicates good and bad emotions to me					
I regularly use my intuition when making decisions					
I regularly reflect on my actions and remind myself how I was feeling at the time of my action					
I know how emotions such as anger, happiness, sadness, fear and guilt are expressed by my body					
People who are close to me would describe me as emotionally aware, paying careful attention to how positive and negative emotions are expressed by my body					

Total score (out of 40) _____

Figure 5.3 Self-awareness questionnaire

Part 4: Awareness of others

Questions	5 ☺☺	4 ☺	3 Average	2 ☹	1 ☹☹
I regularly try to pay attention to how other people are feeling					
I am good at listening to others, and rarely interrupt them					
I am usually aware of other people's body language					
I regularly check with others how they are feeling by asking them					
I tend to ask other people lots of open questions as I believe it will help me to understand them better					
I usually notice when someone else is uncomfortable with something, even when they don't say it					
I listen carefully to the words people choose to use, noticing when they use more emotional words like 'never' or 'always'					
I am usually aware of changes in people's voice volume, tone and intonation, reflecting on how their voice expresses their feelings at the time					

Total score (out of 40) _____

Figure 5.4 Awareness of others questionnaire

The maximum score on each scale is 40. Rather than categorizing your score as 'good' or 'bad', it is better to think that if the score on any of the four scales is below 35, then you could benefit from engaging with the activities in this chapter. We will start by looking at developing your self-regard and regard for others.

SELF-REGARD

First, let's just remind ourselves what self-regard actually is: *it is about how much you accept and value yourself as a person*. Accepting and valuing ourselves is essential for good health, happiness and success. It is also something needed, directly or indirectly, for all the components of emotional intelligence.

Beware! Sometimes people appear to have high self-regard but in fact have developed an 'act'. There are two simple tests to check if this is the case. If your self-regard is genuinely high you will also genuinely empathize with and accept others even when they are very different from you (regard for others). Also, if your self-regard is genuinely high you will be accurately aware of your strengths and weaknesses and regularly invite honest feedback about your actions from others. A person with genuinely high self-regard will welcome constructive feedback from others. Rather than feeling threatened by it or defending against it, he or she will see it as an opportunity for developing and learning.

The following example demonstrates how self-regard can impact on performance at work.

Julie and the PowerPoint presentation

Julie is new in her job at a large accountancy firm. During the first week she is asked to prepare and deliver a short PowerPoint presentation to a group of potential customers. As Julie has never done this before, she becomes very anxious about the task, but feels she cannot ask anyone for help as she wants to create a good impression. Instead, she buys herself a book on PowerPoint and spends long hours after work trying to teach herself how to give an effective presentation using this tool.

On the day of the presentation Julie is very nervous. This clearly shows during her talk as she seems unclear and anxious in front of her audience. This is supported by the negative feedback given by the group. Julie goes home feeling like a failure. She has not performed well in her first week of work and she begins to ask herself if she is really good enough to work for this company.

What do you think Julie did wrong and how does this relate to her level of self-regard?

Discussion

Julie's problems could stem from a low level of self-regard. People with high levels of self-regard value and accept themselves for who they are, and are clearly able to separate this from tasks and activities. They are also able to readily admit if they can't do something.

It is perfectly acceptable that Julie does not know how to present and how to use PowerPoint. Julie is Julie and whatever she is and isn't able to do is ok! If she had a high level of self-regard, she may have:

- happily taken on the task and viewed it as an opportunity to develop some new skills;
- admitted that she did not know how to use PowerPoint and asked colleagues with more experience for help;
- accepted that in only a week she was not going to deliver a perfect presentation, but that this is ok;
- asked for and been open to constructive feedback from the group after her presentation so she can learn from it and improve next time.

Self-regard activity 1

Being honest about skills and mistakes

Think of a time when you acted like Julie, and said you could do something you were not confident about but did not ask for help. What did you think, feel and do at this time?

Think:
Feel:
Do:

Now rewrite the think, feel and do, inserting how you would be different next time this happens. Remember to separate what you can do from who you are.

Self-regard activity 2

Two of me!

One way of looking at genuine self-regard and avoiding confusing it with your actions is to think of separating yourself into two different people, as in the following activity.

Imagine splitting yourself into two separate people. On the left is the person who you are. Here, you should list all the qualities you have that are not conditional. For example: I am flexible, trustworthy and am really good at understanding others.

On the right, list what you do (eg, achievements and abilities). For example, I am a qualified engineer, I am a great tennis player. For the list of your qualities, feel free to ask friends, colleagues and loved ones to contribute. Do not stop compiling this list until you have at least 15 key qualities in the 'Who I am' column.

Who I am (self-esteem)   What I do (self-confidence)

Self-regard activity 3

Your daily self-regard workout: feeding your lion

Most of us are happy to give up 10 minutes a day to physical exercise, but what about exercising our brain? Remember, unless we feed it and tame it, our lion (unconscious emotional brain) will always take over our thinking and actions. This daily workout will help your lion tamer (conscious thinking brain) to tame the lion, feeding it positive thoughts to get each day off to a great start. The activity should only take about 10 minutes and, although it can be done at any time, it is recommended you do it in the mornings before starting the day ahead.

Find a quiet, undisturbed space with a mirror. Look at yourself in the mirror and repeat the following steps:

1. Keeping your eyes open and looking at yourself in the mirror, spend one minute completing the following sentence, using only positive, unconditional praise (positive things about who you are, not what you do): 'I like me because. . .'.
2. Thank yourself for the praise.
3. For one minute, close your eyes and picture yourself in a memory when you were relaxed, confident and happy. See how you were behaving, remember what you were thinking, and feel how you felt at the time.
4. Count backwards from 10 to 1.
5. Keeping your eyes closed, remember a specific time when you were paid a compliment by someone you respect and trust. Repeat what happened in specific detail, remembering how you felt at the time. Focus on this positive feeling and imagine it getting bigger and bigger.
6. Open your eyes and look at yourself. Allow yourself to see what the other person saw and repeat it to yourself.

7. Now think of your day ahead. Spend one minute thinking how you will use your qualities and positive feelings to help you be successful and enjoy the day ahead, seeing any challenges as opportunities for growth and learning rather than problems to be concerned about.
8. Repeat step 1 just before you go to bed each evening.

Top tip: if you repeat this activity at roughly the same time each day the habit of doing it will form more quickly. Why not link it to another habit you already have, like cleaning your teeth?

Self-regard activity 4

Challenging your conditional self-regard

It might be worth taking a moment to work out your own conditions of worth. Make a list of the conditions you put on yourself that, in your mind, make you ok as a person.

Here are some possible conditions of worth you may identify with yourself, but feel free to add any of your own:

I am ok as long as. . . .

- I am perfect.
- I help others.
- I am busy.
- I have lots of friends.
- I have my family.
- I have my husband/wife/partner.
- I control others.
- I have a big house
- I live in the right district.
- I have a big car.
- I go to the best holiday resorts.
- I wear expensive, designer clothes.
- I dine at expensive restaurants.
- I am successful.
- I always win.

Now make your own list.

'I am ok because I am me.' What would it take for you to believe this statement?

For each of the conditions of worth you have written down, reflect on the last time you used this condition of worth to try to feel better about yourself. Now replace these with thoughts of unconditional praise for yourself. Cross out each of the items on the above list and rewrite your conditions of worth with positive unconditional statements. For example, I am ok because:

- I am flexible.
- I am funny.
- I am reliable and trustworthy.
- I am supportive and helpful.

What are strokes?

Our self-regard is made up of a complicated mixture of attitudes that lie in our unconscious, emotional brain – our lion. Like any animal, to stay healthy our lion needs to be regularly fed the right food. When someone else gives us some feedback, it feeds our lion, sometimes giving it healthy food that will help it to grow, other times giving it unhealthy food that will have a negative impact on the lion. Psychologists refer to these units of feedback from others as 'strokes'. Strokes may be verbal ('I love working with you') or non-verbal (a warm smile when someone you like enters the room). For our self-regard to develop and remain healthy, it needs positive strokes from other people. In contrast, regular negative strokes from others can reduce our levels of self-regard.

There are four types of strokes we can receive from others (and ourselves if we listen to our inner voice); these are shown in Figure 5.5. You will notice that we have given each of these stroke boxes 'scores', which give an indication of the impact they can have on our self-regard. For example, a -10 can have a big negative impact on our self-regard, but a +10 can have a big positive impact on our self-regard.

Negative unconditional strokes are always unacceptable, and as a result we have given them a -10 on the self-regard balance. It is never useful to criticize someone for who he or she is and, if that person accepts this stroke and lets it in, it will always have a negative impact on his or her self-regard. Often negative unconditional strokes are not stated verbally, but implied by non-verbal communication. For example, the manager who puts a report on your desk and tells you it needs to be rewritten while rolling his or her eyes and shaking his or her head is delivering the message: 'I think you are useless' or, 'It doesn't surprise me, you are pretty stupid.'

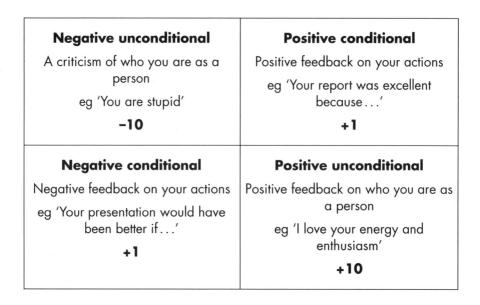

Figure 5.5 The strokes grid

Negative conditional strokes are sometimes necessary and, when given in a constructive way, are useful. They are feedback on a person's behaviour, such as, 'Your presentation would have had more impact if you varied your voice tone more' or, 'It would be more effective if you added more pictures to your slides.' These strokes are useful as they build on our learning and development. To be effective, they must be specific and constructive. A comment like, 'Your presentation needs to improve' is not much use to the recipient as it doesn't teach anything. A simple rule when giving negative conditional strokes is that unless you can be specific and suggest constructive improvements, keep your mouth shut!

Positive conditional strokes are also useful, again provided they are specific. They focus on praising something you have done, such as, 'Your report was great; it was clearly written, concise and focused on the key issues.' Like negative conditionals, they are useful as they build on learning and development.

Positive unconditionals are the strokes which, if accepted, will have the biggest positive impact on your self-regard. They involve praising you for who you are, not what you have done. Examples could be, 'I love working with you because you are always so positive' or, 'I always feel relaxed when working with you.' We have given these a +10 score on the self-regard balance, because they feel great when you receive them and provide your lion with the perfect food for healthy growth.

Stop a moment and think about what types of strokes are used at your workplace or in your business. Are you promoting and developing people's self-regard, or does your work culture regularly chip away at people's self-regard, leaving people feeling unhappy and demotivated?

Self-regard activity 5

Learning to manage your strokes

Strokes will only have a positive or negative impact on our self-regard if we allow them to. If we want to manage the strokes we receive effectively, we need to develop the habit of rejecting negative unconditional strokes and accepting positive unconditional strokes.

How do you normally react when you receive negative strokes? Do you dwell on them? Do you sometimes blow up negative conditionals, and interpret negative comments about your actions as criticism of you as a person?

What about positive strokes? Do you get embarrassed when people praise you or your actions? Do you find excuses such as, 'I was lucky' or, 'It's my job to do well'? How easy do you find it to accept compliments?

Part 1: Rejecting negative unconditional strokes
Think of any time you received negative unconditional strokes. How did you think, feel and behave at the time?

Relive the situation in your mind, this time clearly rejecting the negative stroke you were given and turning it into a positive (eg 'I am not stupid, I am intelligent.')

Part 2: Accepting positive strokes
Think of a time you received positive unconditional strokes. How did you think, feel and behave at the time?

Relive the situation in your head; accepting the positive stroke you were given. Acknowledge it by saying 'Thank you' to the person and then repeat this stroke several times in your head, each time agreeing with it and acknowledging it by saying thank you.

How do you feel right now?
Repeat these two activities, spending 10 minutes per day on them every day for the next three weeks. During this time, notice how you respond differently to strokes you receive from others.

Part 3: Giving yourself positive unconditional strokes by advertising yourself
Most of us are very modest about our qualities and strengths. The society we live in often encourages us to put ourselves down rather than praising ourselves. This activity is designed to allow you the time and space to focus on your positive qualities.

Design an advertisement for yourself that will sell you and your qualities as a person. Focus on who you are and what makes you a great person, not on what you do and your achievements. Your advert can be a written description, a poem, a picture or anything you want it to be – as long as it specifically shows a number of your strengths. Make sure you include a minimum of 10 qualities that you have.

When you are happy with what you have created, spend 10 minutes presenting it out loud, either to some people you trust and value or, if you'd prefer, to an imaginary audience on your own.

REGARD FOR OTHERS

What is regard for others?

It is the degree to which you accept and value others as people. This is clearly distinct from liking or approving of what they may do. In other words, you don't have to like the actions, but you respect the person behind the actions.

Dishonest Kate

Kate is a liar. She sees no problem in telling small lies (or 'alternative versions of the truth' as she calls them) to get what she wants. She is part of a three-person sales team, where it is important the team members 'work as one' to achieve the best results. Kate's colleagues are Julie and Sam. Although Kate is very careful not to lie to customers, she is happy to lie to her husband. She regularly shares tales of an affair she is having with her fellow team members. The problem is, while Julie doesn't mind, Sam has really started to dislike Kate since she started having the affair. She hates the fact that she is disloyal to her husband and is finding it increasingly hard to listen to Kate's stories of deception. Eventually, the dishonesty gets too much for Sam and she decides she has to leave the team – she can no longer continue to work with 'such a horrible person'.

The problem here is a combination of values and emotionally unintelligent behaviour. For Julie, honesty is not an important value, so Kate's lies do not evoke a strong emotional reaction in her. However, honesty is a core value for Sam, so each time she hears Kate's stories she reacts strongly. The strong negative emotions Sam feels influence her thinking and result in her making a moral judgement of Julie ('a horrible person'). What gives Sam the right to judge Julie? How can she brand her as a horrible person?

The problem with judgement is that it clouds understanding. As soon as you make a judgement of a situation or person, you may stop understanding them. Obviously, Sam has every right to value honesty and feel the negative emotions she does when Kate is dishonest. What's wrong here is the judgement that follows these emotions. She can't really know that Kate is a horrible person, and how do you measure what is horrible and not horrible anyhow?

Regard for others activity 1

Separate the person from the actions

Just as with self-regard, having high regard for others involves being able to separate people (who they are) from their actions (what they do).

Behaviour can be criticized, people can't! Think of a situation when you were critical of another person. Try to remember:

- the thoughts you had at the time;
- how you felt at the time;
- what you did at the time.

Now imagine splitting the person you criticized into two separate people. On the left is the person, who he or she is. On the right are his or her actions or opinions that you disagreed with.

Take a sheet of paper and split it into two columns, headed 'Who they are' and 'What they did'. Fill in the columns with all the criticisms you thought about this person. For example, a thought like, 'You are such an unreliable person' would go into the 'Who they are' list, but, 'What you did was so unreliable' would go into the 'What they did' list. Now repeat this activity for two more people you have criticized.

How many comments have you got in the 'Who they are' list? For each of these comments, cross them out and rewrite them in the 'What they did' list, changing each one to focus on specific behaviours.

Regard for others activity 2

Recognizing your ok patterns

In Chapter 3 we looked at the 'Ok corral' – the attitudes you have about valuing yourself and others; see Fig 5.6.

For each of the four boxes, think of one real-life situation when you feel you were in that box and write down what you thought, how you felt and what you did at that time. An example is shown in Figure 5.7.

I'm not ok You're ok Passive	I'm ok You're ok Healthy Assertive
I'm not ok You're not ok Stuck Passive-aggressive	I'm ok You're not ok Judgemental Aggressive

Figure 5.6   The ok corral

I'm not ok You're ok	I'm ok You're ok
Situation: Had argument with my best friend **Thought:** He doesn't like me anymore **Felt:** Nervous, sad, disappointed, irritated **Did:** Sat and worried for 2 days, did not call him as worried he would be annoyed if I bothered him	**Situation:** Discussed pay rise with my boss **Thought:** I deserve more money but understand she is running a business **Felt:** Excited, energised, comfortable **Did:** Asked her assertively and explained clearly why, and also listened to her arguments. (We compromised on my original request)
I'm not ok You're not ok	**I'm ok You're not ok**
Situation: I was made redundant **Thought:** I'm not good enough, my boss didn't like me **Felt:** Uncomfortable, disappointed, sad, hopeless **Did:** Nothing for 2 weeks. Sat around feeling sorry for myself and didn't look for new jobs as I didn't see the point trying	**Situation:** Somebody pushed in front of me in a queue **Thought:** What an idiot! **Felt:** Irritated, angry **Did:** Shouted loudly, "there is a queue here, get to the back."

Figure 5.7   The ok corral: example

Once you have completed your own table in all four boxes, rewrite the three unhealthy boxes in Figure 5.8 ('I'm not ok, you're ok'; 'I'm ok, you're not ok'; 'I'm not ok, you're not ok').

I'm not ok **You're ok**	**I'm ok** **You're ok**
Situation: Thought: Felt: Did:	Situation: Thought: Felt: Did:
I'm not ok **You're not ok**	**I'm ok** **You're not ok**
Situation: Thought: Felt: Did:	Situation: Thought: Felt: Did:

Figure 5.8 The ok corral: rewrite the 'unhealthy' boxes

For each of them, rewrite what your thoughts, feelings and actions would have been if you were in the healthy 'I'm ok; you're ok', position at the time it happened:

▓   How would your thoughts have been different? What feelings would you have had? How would your behaviour have been more effective?
▓   What have you learnt from this activity?
▓   How will you use this in future?
▓   What action will you take to make sure you live more of your life in the healthy 'I'm ok, you're ok' position?

- How can you apply this at work or in your business?
- How can you use it at home?

Regard for others activity 3

Stepping into someone else's shoes

Find a quiet place where you can be alone for at least 10 minutes. Think of a situation where you had an argument or disagreement with someone. Your eyes should remain closed throughout this activity, so read through it all first and then try to remember the steps. If you find this difficult, ask someone to read them out to you as you do the activity.

Visualize, in as much detail as possible, what happened at the time. Try to relive the situation in your head now, remembering what you thought, how you felt and how you acted. *Count backwards from 10 to 1.*

Go back to the same situation again, but this time try to put yourself in the head and body of the other person. What is he or she thinking? What emotions is he or she feeling? What is he or she doing? *Count backwards from 10 to 1.*

Now relive the situation for a third time, but this time you are watching the argument as a neutral bystander. Observe carefully how both you and the other person are behaving. What are you saying? How is the other person responding? What are you doing with your body language? How about the other person? How effectively are you managing your emotions? *Count backwards from 10 to 1.*

Now open your eyes and write down the answers to the following questions:

- What have you learnt from this activity?
- What do you understand better about the other person now?
- What do you understand better about yourself now?
- If the situation were to happen again, what would you do differently?

SELF-AWARENESS

Self-awareness is the degree to which you are in touch with your body, your feelings and your intuition.

How can you develop self-awareness?

Feelings do not live in the brain; they are whole-body experiences. That's why we have expressions such as 'get hot under the collar', 'gut feeling' and 'cold feet'. Consequently, increasing our awareness of our feeling states and our intuition involves learning to pay more attention to, and to attune ourselves to, what is going on in our body and how this affects our behaviour.

We can feel when we have done the right thing. Likewise, we know when we have done something that does not sit well with us. Our emotional brain will communicate this via feelings or sensations experienced around the body. This is intuition. Our intuition can't communicate in words, so it has to find another way. This could be increasing the tension in our muscles, headaches, an uncomfortable feeling in the stomach, loss of appetite, sleepless nights and many more physical signs. If we are in touch with our emotions and listen to them (self-awareness), they will tell us whether what we have done is right or wrong. The problem is, our thinking brain is good at deceiving us. The following example demonstrates how this can happen.

An important business decision

Jesper is a negotiator. He has an important position in the procurement division of his company. He has to purchase 20,000 new valves for an important piece of equipment his company produces. He has been in negotiations with two key sellers. Seller A sells the valves at a unit price of 15 euros, Seller B at 13 euros. After several meetings with both sellers, Jesper notices that he always feels energized when he has met with Seller A – the meetings just seem to fly by. In contrast, he always comes away from meetings with Seller B feeling drained and with an uncomfortable, nervous feeling in his stomach. After much thought, Jesper persuades himself to ignore the feelings and to do the rational thing; go for Seller B with the cheaper unit price: 'This is business after all.'

For several weeks after the decision Jesper continued to feel uncomfortable and anxious about the new supplier. After three months of cooperation the supplier stopped replying to Jesper's calls and, eventually, when Jesper managed to track him down, explained that they were experiencing staffing problems and would not be able to meet the supply of the valves for the next two months.

Would you have done the same? Was Jesper right? One thing is certain here: Jesper failed to listen to his emotional brain or intuition. Trust is an important value to Jesper and his intuition was telling him that there was something about Seller B he didn't trust. Jesper chose to ignore these clear signals and ended up paying the price. Have you ever done this? When was the last time you allowed your logical brain to persuade you to go against your intuition? What price did you pay?

Self-awareness is about being in touch with your feeling states and intuition. It is the key to acting with emotional intelligence. In order to be in the habit of listening to what your emotional brain is telling you, you need to have a high level of self-awareness.

Self-awareness activity 1

Understanding your intuition

When you experience something inconsistent with your core values, you are likely to have strong negative emotions. This intuitive sense of what is right and wrong is an invaluable guide we all have. Of course, it is only useful if you listen to it. Emotionally intelligent people are in tune with their intuition and use it to make important decisions.

Try asking yourself the following questions:

- How does my intuition communicate to me?
- When was the last time I had a strong intuitive feeling?
- Where did I feel it in my body?
- When was the last time I acted on my intuition?
- How often do I use my intuition when making important decisions?

Doing things right becomes much easier when you understand your core values and learn to listen to your intuition. Understanding your own core values will also help you to understand why you make moral judgements of others. Each time somebody does or says something that does not fit with one of our own core values, we are more likely to jump into the 'I'm ok, you're not ok' box and judge them.

Self-awareness activity 2

Three steps to increasing self-awareness

Self-awareness is about recognizing when we are experiencing a feeling or emotion inside. Once you have done this you need to label this emotion and then manage the emotion so that you can choose how to behave:

Step 1: Recognize that we have a feeling.
Step 2: Be able to give the emotion a name.
Step 3: Acknowledge the emotion and choose how to behave.

Think of a situation where you had a strong emotional reaction to something. Now go through the three steps and work out what the emotion was, and how it impacted on your thoughts and behaviour. How will this increased self-awareness help you in future?

Self-awareness activity 3

Identifying emotions

If you find it difficult to identify your emotions, this activity may help. Practise becoming aware of the feelings in your body. For example, when did you last get that uncomfortable feeling in your stomach? When did you last get an adrenalin rush? When did you last feel stressed and where did it show in your body?

Sometimes the effects of our emotions are obvious, at other times they can be more subtle. Here are some examples to get you started:

When you...	you often...
have a near miss when driving	get hot and your neck muscles feel tense
are embarrassed	go red in the face and laugh
are frustrated	start fidgeting in your chair
are in physical danger	start to shake and feel cold
are angry	raise your voice and feel warm

Look at each of the following situations and, if you have ever experienced them, try to identify the emotion and behaviour you experienced at the time:

Situation	Emotion/reaction
When...	you often...
one of your colleagues fails to say 'good morning' to you	
you nearly hit someone or something in your car	
you do something clumsy	
you are criticized for some work you have done	
you are given praise for some work you have done	
you are late for a meeting	
someone else is late for a meeting	
your plane is delayed by two hours	
you are asked to do a task you find boring	
you lose interest in something	

Self-awareness activity 4

Learning from the past

This exercise aims to identify your earlier life experiences that may still be affecting your behaviour. The following example demonstrates how this could happen.

Tim and trust

Tim used to trust openly. He had been brought up to believe that people were good and always had the best intentions. As a result, Tim entered into a business partnership without a contract and, six months later, his partner stole all his ideas and set up on his own. Tim was devastated – how could someone be so cruel?

Three years later Tim had set up again on his own and his new business was doing well. Despite advice from his colleagues that it could do even better by entering into a partnership, Tim was strongly against this idea. Just the mention of partnership created a sinking feeling in Tim's stomach and he became irritable and snappy.

Reflect on experiences from earlier in your life that had a big emotional impact on you. Consider how these experiences may still be affecting your feelings and/or your behaviour today. Write your thoughts, feelings and behaviours down under the two headings:

Experience   **Continuing effects today**

Once you've identified these experiences you can talk them over with someone you trust such as a close friend or relative. Now close your eyes and visualize the original experience. Remember where you were, how you felt and what you thought.

Now change the setting, and make it someone more pleasant and relaxing. Add some positive music to the scene, something energizing and happy. Now change what you and the other people in the scene are wearing. You are now dressed in a clown's costume, dancing around and enjoying the music and atmosphere.

How do you feel about the situation right now?

AWARENESS OF OTHERS

Do other people matter to you? Are you really interested in what they have to say and are you concerned for their wellbeing?

There are a number of skills we can learn that will help us to improve our awareness of others. Remember, however, you are only likely to be motivated to improve your awareness of others if you have a high regard for others and genuinely want to understand them better. Here we will look at three broad areas you can develop:

1. Empathy skills;
2. Listening skills;
3. Questioning skills.

As we will discuss in Chapter 7, these are also the core skills necessary to be an effective coach. We will now look at activities to develop empathy, listening and questioning skills.

1. Empathy

What is empathy?

We believe empathy is the building block for positive relationships and the ability and motivation to recognize and respond to other people's fears, concerns and feelings. Empathy is:

- trying to see things from the other person's point of view;
- not making assumptions about the other person;
- not judging other people;
- trying hard to appreciate another person's perspective.

If you fail to be empathic the following will be common:

- People will resent you because they feel you are insensitive.
- Communication is difficult; people don't want to talk to you and you don't want to listen.
- You give poor or no feedback to people.
- You rarely give praise to people.
- You regularly fail to anticipate others' needs.
- You regularly jump to conclusions.

Daniel Goleman refers to empathy as our 'social radar'. As the majority of communication is non-verbal, to be truly empathic it is important to be highly attuned to body language clues, voice changes and facial expressions.

Awareness of others activity 1

Developing your empathy level

Use the checklist in Table 5.1 to identify where your empathy skills are high and if there are any areas you could improve. For each area, decide whether you are good – you do this regularly; average – you sometimes do this but could improve; or poor – you rarely or never do this.

Table 5.1 Empathy questionnaire

Behaviour/Awareness	Poor	Average	Good
Avoid interrupting others			
Ask how other people are feeling			
Acknowledge people's feelings			
Tackle anger or negative feelings well			
Are comfortable with silences			
Are aware when other people are uncomfortable			
Invite others to express their feelings			
Are comfortable with closeness and affection			
Avoid jumping to conclusions about how others feel			
Pick up and read others' body language			
Feel comfortable when others express their feelings			
Ask mainly open questions			
Total			

For those where you scored yourself average or poor, make a priority list of around three concrete things you will focus on doing more of for the next three weeks. After each day, take a couple of minutes to review if you have succeeded in improving your actions. After three weeks, evaluate where your empathy levels are again by repeating the whole questionnaire. It would also be useful to get a colleague or friend to complete the questionnaire before and after the three weeks, to see if they have noticed any changes in your empathy-related behaviour.

2. Listening

Awareness of others activity 2

Removing your barriers to listening

The first thing to be aware of with effective listening is the barriers that get in the way.

What stops you from being an effective listener? Give yourself a score from 1 to 10 on each of the barriers to listening shown in Table 5.2, with 1 being a low score (rarely) and 10 being a high score.

Table 5.2 Listening questionnaire

Do you. . .

1. Get distracted by inner thoughts that are nothing to do with what the other person is saying?

2. Stop listening because you are planning what to say next?

3. Start labelling the other person based on what he or she is saying?

4. Listen only through the filter of your existing knowledge of the person?

5. Interrupt the other person?

6. Stop the other person from following his or her own train of thought?

7. Sit so that the other person has difficulty maintaining eye contact?

8. Give the person good non-verbal attention?

9. Fail to match the other person's body language?

10. Allow what is going on around you to distract your attention?

11. Apply labels by saying things like 'Well, he's a man, isn't he?'

12. Preach – just tell the other person what to do?

13. Diagnose too soon and provide what you think is the right answer?

14. Dismiss others' concerns as silly or irrelevant?

15. Offer clichés such as 'What's meant to be is meant to be?'

16. Trivialize the matter by telling the person it's really not worth getting upset about?

17. Offer false reassurance such as 'Don't worry, I'm sure it will never come to that!'?

18. Show impatience when the other person takes time to explain their situation?

19. Collude, when challenging is more appropriate, saying things like 'Yes, you're right, everyone knows that women are unpredictable?

20. Not accept the other person's feelings, saying things like 'That's a stupid way to feel?'

21. Turn the conversation around so that it becomes about you, not the other person?

For the next three weeks, focus your attention on the low-scoring behaviour(s) when listening to others. Challenge and change the behaviour each day and write down how you feel you have improved your listening after each day.

What have been the benefits of doing this? What other listening behaviours can you focus on improving?

Awareness of others activity 3

Using different levels of listening

When we listen to others, we can generally do it on three levels:

1. Factual listening (focus on facts the other person is telling you).
2. Emotional (focus on the other person's emotions and non-verbal cues).
3. Intuitive listening (focus on your own emotions and intuition).

Factual listening is, as the name suggests, listening for facts. This may be particularly useful when trying to make arrangements, for example. The focus is often on you and getting the information you need.

Emotional listening is more attentive and requires more effort. Here you are listening for emotions, feelings, tone of voice and pauses. This is the level of listening to use most when you are really trying to understand the other person.

Intuitive listening is the most difficult. This level of listening happens at the unconscious level and can often be heard as your 'gut instinct'. For example, can you think of a time when someone was describing his or her job to you and telling you how much he or she loved it, but something inside you didn't feel right? Being aware of this intuition would perhaps enable you to ask people more about their jobs and what they felt about them.

Next time you are listening to someone, pay attention to the type of listening you find easiest to use. Are you particularly focused on facts? Do you tend to notice emotions and forget details? Are you more aware of what is going on inside you rather than paying attention to the other person?

For the level of listening you find the most challenging, focus on improving this over the next two to three weeks, spending a few moments to evaluate how well you feel you have listened to someone after a conversation.

3. Questioning

Asking the right type of question is a crucial skill to help develop your understanding of others. It will not only help to resolve arguments constructively, it will also help you to encourage other people to speak when they are reluctant to.

Awareness of others activity 4

The two-minute open question challenge

How much of the time do you spend asking open questions and avoid falling into the habit of asking closed questions? Closed questions, as the name suggests, will encourage other people to be closed and will therefore be of little use to you if you are trying to understand others better. Here is a simple challenge you can set yourself today. Spend two minutes asking someone only open questions. The first time you ask a closed question within the two minutes, you have failed in your task. Sounds easy doesn't it?

Repeat the challenge every day for the next three weeks. Monitor how successfully you find the challenge each day. Is it getting any easier? Are you starting to change your questioning style habits?

Who is the question for?

Most of the time we ask other people questions because we want information that we can use. However, it can often be more valuable to ask other people questions that will help them to get more information they can use.

Summary

- Your EI is not fixed and is completely changeable.
- It takes 21 days to change a habit.
- Who do you talk to most in your life? Yourself! So make sure it's positive!
- Remember to accept yourself (and others) for who you (they) are and not for what you (they) do.
- Pay attention to your feelings – they're trying to tell you something.
- Practise empathy with others – it will make a big difference to the quality of your relationships.
- Listening is a gift.
- Keep a check on the strokes you give and take on board for yourself.
- Remember, judgement is the enemy of understanding.
- Fine tune your intuition; it's a powerful tool indeed.

6

Understanding and working with values, beliefs and attitudes

> *It is never too late to be what you might have been.*
>
> George Eliot

INSIDE-OUT PERFORMANCE

Imagine building a house without the foundations in place, imagine having a garden landscaped without the right quality soil and fertilizer, and imagine planting a tree without the roots. What would happen? Your house may crack or even collapse over time, your garden will not flourish and the tree will die. So getting the right foundations, roots and fertilizer is all about understanding and working with your values, beliefs and attitudes.

To start this chapter, here are a few questions for you:

- What really motivates you? What are your values?
- What are your key attitudes that create your daily behaviour and habits?
- What kind of beliefs do you hold – are they positive and inspiring you to take action or do they hold you back?

Can you answer these easily or do you need to think about them? Chances are you will probably have to really give these questions some thought. Why? Our values, beliefs and attitudes all live within the emotional, unconscious part of our brain, and for many that's where they stay. Yet the best way to increase your performance is to have a look inside and discover how your values, attitudes and beliefs can support you. So first of all, let's look at what values, beliefs and attitudes actually are.

What are values?

Imagine having a compass for your life or a treasure map where X marks the spot, (X being the treasure chest with your values inside), which helps you recognize who you really are. That's what having and knowing your values is like. Values are hugely important: they're your personal motivators, they're what make you tick and the greatest tragedy is that most people go through life not even knowing they've got values, let alone what they are. They are like having your own internal compass and when you pay attention to them, they give you direction in life. Hyrum Smith (2001) defines values as, 'what we believe to be of the greatest importance and highest priority in our lives.'

It's also important to understand that values are not:

- tangible, nor are they physical objects (money is not a value but what it represents to people is, eg security, independence, success);
- needs (necessities in life, as described by Maslow, 1954, in his hierarchy of needs);
- ethics (agreed codes of behaviour);
- morals (right and wrong, good and bad);
- judgements (labels that come from our beliefs about life, people, situations);
- attitudes or beliefs, though they do live in the same brain (the emotional brain/limbic system).

What are beliefs?

Do you believe in Santa Claus? Do you believe the world is round or flat? Whatever you answer, that is what you 'believe' to be true. The dictionary defines a belief as 'an idea, a principle accepted as true, especially without proof.' Beliefs are an expression of the degree of certainty we have about something. The key with beliefs is that they are not necessarily correct. A classic example here is that for thousands of years we believed the earth was flat and we now know that it's a sphere. Our beliefs represent our 'truth' or our 'story of the world'. It is important to recognize that we all have different stories, different truths. There is a difference in 'truth' for individuals and there is a definite difference in 'truth' between cultures. John Whitmore talks about how 'the story that a coach has needs to be pretty sophisticated, and he or she needs to be broad and deep in consciousness'. Think about what your beliefs are doing for you. Are they supporting you to achieve your goals or holding you back?

What are attitudes?

We believe that attitudes are things in our unconscious emotional brain that are linked to our emotions and behaviours (eg, I'm not good enough, I'm good enough). The dictionary defines attitudes as 'the way a person views something or tends to behave towards it, often in an evaluative way'. In *Applied EI* the definition used is 'an evaluative position that we hold about a thing, a person, an idea or perhaps an organization'.

What's the difference between attitudes and beliefs?

We had lots of discussion about this and the research we carried out brought up many conflicting points. We believe that attitudes are whole-body experiences and have a strong connection to our emotions, in a sense, whole-body beliefs. When you see someone for the first time without speaking to them about their thinking, it is much easier to get a sense of their attitudes than their beliefs. Attitudes show up in people's demeanour, their way of being and their energy.

Let's take the example from Chapter 1 of Sally who has an irrational fear of spiders. If you ask her how she feels about them, she gets shivers down her spine and instinctively wants to run out of the room. If you ask her what she believes about spiders, she may not be able to put this into words. This is because she has an irrational fear that comes from an unconscious attitude, which she gets a whole-body sense about, but not logical thought. An attitude is something more than a belief, as it is an emotional expression. Beliefs can form attitudes and attitudes can form beliefs.

Ultimately, attitudes and beliefs can help or hinder us and affect how we behave and how much of our potential we use. As we described in Chapter 1, attitudes are all specific 'default' patterns of neurones wired in our emotional brain. All attitudes can be rewired to form new, healthier attitudes if we choose to do this. The key is to get underneath the ones that undermine us (by first raising conscious awareness of them), weed them out and replace them with healthy supportive beliefs and attitudes (many of the activities in Chapter 5 will help you do this).

A powerful combination!

So, values, attitudes and beliefs have a powerful connection with our thoughts, feelings and behaviours and how we perform. Consider a tree with values representing the roots of who we are, the beliefs being the trunk, attitudes being the main branches with the leaves being our behaviours and actions. Psychologists often talk about values, beliefs and attitudes as similar. We believe that values are an intrinsic part of who we are, and our core values are far less changeable than our beliefs and attitudes.

Let's look at each of these elements in more detail, and explore how they can support you to be the very best version of you, either as a coach or as a coachee.

VALUES

To know your values is a real gift. They help you work out what it is you really want and what motivates you, and explain why you behave/respond like you do on a daily basis.

Have you ever had the situation where something happens at work, and you find it mildly irritating while another colleague hits the roof? You probably thought to yourself, 'That's a bit over the top' or, 'What's the fuss about?' It may be that your colleague has just had a core value stepped on, while it didn't impact yours too much.

When you know your values, when you know what's really important to you, then you can focus on the things you really care about, rather than wasting time on things, people and activities that aren't a priority for you. Sometimes people get too caught up in what they feel they should be doing rather than what they really want to be doing, often imposed by other people. In a sense, being true to your values gives you freedom.

What are your values?

Stop and think about this for a moment: what is really important to you in your life? This is a question we often ask the people we coach and train. The most popular responses are 'my family' and sometimes 'my career', 'my friends' or 'money'. While these are very valid responses, they're not values, but what they represent are. To get under the surface of these priorities, we'd ask the question, 'So what does that give you/bring you?' If we take the example of family, some people will answer 'belonging'; others may respond with 'security, love, nurturing, fun,' etc. If your family is important to you, what is it that they bring you?

Really getting to know and understand your values can take some considerable thought, and coaching is a great way of identifying them. A coach can ask you powerful questions that help you access your emotional brain, rather than the logical brain. We wouldn't give you a list of values to select from as your logical brain could kick in and start 'shopping' for values you feel you should have, be it honesty, fun, or happiness.

Where do values come from?

The answer to this question is still very much under debate. It's the age-old nature/nurture debate. Some people think we're born with them and will argue that they know three siblings who are all very different and yet brought up within the same family, with the same beliefs and surroundings. Other people say that it's more about influences they have throughout life that impact their values. The kind of influences we're talking about here could include family, relatives, teachers, friends at school, media, life experiences, culture, etc. Some research suggests that our core values are in place come late childhood and remain with us throughout our lives, although the priorities do change. Morris Massey (1979), a values theorist, suggests that values evolve during the formative years in a child and only a 'significant emotional event' will change them.

Your uniqueness

We all have a different set of values, in the same way that we all have unique DNA and fingerprints. They're what make us unique and distinct from others. There will never be another human being exactly the same as you on this planet!

Think about relationships you have and what some of the values of the other person/people might be. Do you have some values in common, some values that are very different and some that potentially clash? Maybe there's someone in your life, either at work or within your circle of friends, who you don't seem to get on with and you have no idea why. Maybe, just maybe, it's because he or she has a different set of values to you – understanding that in itself can be releasing and a way to start bridging the gap.

Getting your ducks in a row

James has a set of values that include freedom, independence, adventure and spontaneity. His mother, Aimee, has values that include belonging, nurturing, acceptance, security and love and she is constantly ringing James and wanting to look after him, while his natural inclination is more towards being a free spirit and getting in contact as and when. James often feels frustrated with and a little suffocated by his mum, and sometimes he ignores her calls or snaps at her (and later feels guilty). Aimee feels James is often aloof and angry with her and she feels frustrated, so she calls him all the more.

Who's right and who's wrong?

As behaviour and actions come from values, both James and Aimee find their respective values trampled on at times. To increase their regard for others, it would be helpful if they knew what each other's values were and find a way to reconcile them. This could mean that Aimee restricts her calling to three times a week rather than every day, and that James contacts his mum regularly (and works on managing his emotions to avoid snapping at her).

So, as with the example above, how do you get those ducks in a row and reconcile values that potentially clash? For each party, first of all, there needs to be an awareness of what their own values are (linked to the self-awareness scale) and then an understanding of the values of others (awareness of others). So if James understands what his values are and what his mother's values are, then it's about having regard for his own and his mother's values (self-regard and regard for others), managing his own emotions when his mother next calls (self-management) and communicating his needs/wants in an emotionally intelligent way (relationship management).

We all regularly come into contact with people who have differing values to us and that's something we have to live with and handle. Let's imagine that Aimee makes a habit of contacting James daily. His emotionally intelligent response might be to have an open conversation with her about what's important to him and the fact that daily contact doesn't work for him.

THE IMPACT OF VALUES

Let's first of all consider the impact of your values being out of sync. For example, someone or some situation is stepping on your values; what impact does that have? Here's an example to highlight the impact of values.

The wrong choice?

Susan is fantastic at her job; she's a top sales person in her organization and is recognized with a promotion to sales manager. She receives all the perks that come with the promotion: a healthy pay rise, a beautiful new silver Mercedes company car, health insurance, etc. Her first response is to be delighted, and then gradually over a period of weeks, she begins to feel dissatisfied with life. When Susan looks at this, she thinks how ridiculous she's being. Her bank account has never looked healthier and she's considered a success, and yet there's something missing. Through coaching, Susan identifies that 'making a contribution, achievement, freedom and connection' are really important to her; things that were easily fulfilled in her previous role. However, now sitting in her beautiful office, setting budgets, dealing with customer and staff problems, managing a team of complex characters and attending lots of meetings doesn't feel so appealing. No wonder that she feels dissatisfied; her values are not in line with her actions. So, what does she do? She organizes a meeting with the MD and has an open conversation about how she feels and what would make the difference. It is agreed that she will retain at least two accounts herself, so she still has the connection with clients, can keep some sense of freedom by not sitting in the office all day and can make a contribution with her clients.

How happy do you think Susan feels after the changes?

Knowing your values is good for your health!

When you operate from the healthy life position (I'm ok, you're ok) and are aware of your values, you have a higher regard for others and are more likely to respect the differences you and they have. You are also more likely to take action if your own values are out of balance (showing good self-awareness and self-management). In the example above, Susan dealt with the situation in an emotionally intelligent way; she knew what was missing and was proactive in discussing what would bring her back in line with her values. When you are in line with your values, life will feel easy. By contrast, when your life is out of line with your values you may feel dissatisfied, stressed and, in extreme situations, this can affect your health.

Dean and the stress factor

Dean worked for a large blue-chip company that went through a process of re-organization, which was poorly managed (sound familiar?). The new management were expecting Dean and the team of client directors he worked with to give information to their customers that was blatantly untrue. When he highlighted this to the new managing director, he was told that was the way it was and to deal with it. In short, Dean was expected to behave out of line with his core value of integrity, and over a period of two months this had a negative impact on his health.

He'd tried to overcompensate with his clients by working extremely late and doing far more than the job required. When Dean went for a general health check at his doctor's surgery he was advised that his blood pressure was dangerously high and he was immediately signed off work.

This is an extreme example of what can happen if the way you behave is inconsistent with your values over a long period of time.

Are all values healthy?

The answer to this is yes, provided they are in balance. Most values have a three-dimensional element to them. What does that mean? Let's take the example of Sally, a manager working in the NHS, who has a strong value of 'caring'.

Sally and caring

Sally is feeling tired and drained with her job and things are really getting her down. When she worked with a coach on her values, 'caring' came top of her list. Consider the three sides of caring, shown in Figure 6.1.

Figure 6.1   Values triangle – caring

The coach asked Sally the following questions:

- How well do you care for others?
- How good are you at asking for help/accepting help from others?
- How well do you look after yourself?

Sally said that she was very caring and spent most of her time caring for other people, especially her patients and family. This was what was tiring her out! When Sally was asked the other two questions, any idea what she said? She never asked for help and so everyone thought she was ok and probably didn't need help. As for looking after herself, she just didn't have the time!

A classic example of a value out of balance.

WHY VALUES MATTER

There are huge benefits to knowing your values and those of others. Here's a sample of what coachees and organizations have said about this:

> I understand myself so much better and recognize why I've responded to events/people in my life the way I have.
> I appreciate the differences that my boss and I have, and understand that her values are different from mine and both are equally valid.
> Understanding values has helped us resolve conflict within the department. Now there's an understanding and respect that we each have a right to live according to our own values and can find ways to communicate that respect all parties.
> I've set myself goals and now appreciate why they haven't always worked out; they weren't in line with my values. I now use my values as a solid basis for my goals and always check that the goals I set are firmly in line with them. If they're not, I'm setting myself up to fail.
> Whenever I have a decision to make, I run it past my values and make sure the action I take is compatible with them. Otherwise it's going to be uncomfortable.
> Values are one of the best decision-making tools I've come across. When considering the options, I always ask myself, 'If I do x, does it take me closer to or further away from my values? If I do y, does it take me closer to or further away from my values?' If it takes me further away and I take that choice anyway, I know it's going to be a bumpy ride.
> We have used values as part of our recruitment drive. We know what type of person will fit within our team and we act accordingly.

In short, the benefits of being aware of values include:

- Greater self-awareness – knowing what makes you tick.
- Increased awareness and understanding of others (respecting the differences).

- Solid foundations for your goals. Stephen Covey (1999) talks about people climbing to the top of their ladder, only to find it's leaning up against the wrong wall. Knowing your values avoids this.
- Having access to a great decision-making tool.

The ultimate test

'The ultimate test' is how Peter F Drucker (2007), the world renowned economist, defines values. In his book he describes an event in his life when he was an investment banker in London, which clearly fitted with his strengths and yet didn't fit with his value of 'making a contribution'. He realized how important people were to him and so he quit, despite having no money, no job and no prospects (this was the 1930s and during the Great Depression). He'd taken the ultimate test and made his decision accordingly.

THE ROLE OF VALUES WITHIN COACHING

Values are an essential part of coaching. Let's consider the two perspectives of coach and coachee.

We have talked in previous chapters about the importance of developing your emotional intelligence as a coach. It is essential that you have high self-regard or you might not take the necessary action to ensure you're living in line with your values. The importance of operating from the' healthy' life position box as a coach should not be underestimated. When you know your own values, you are operating from an informed place about what works ' for you and being true to that when you are coaching others. You may also need to consider in what situations you wouldn't coach (be it individuals or organizations) if there is a strong clash with your own values. For example, would you be happy to coach within a nuclear power organization or within the tobacco industry?

Working with coachees to identify their values can bring enormous benefits to them and to your working relationship. When you are working with coachees who have defined their values, they could be used effectively within the relationship to regularly check about the right course of action or mode of operation for them.

Interpretation

It is important to remember that values can mean different things to different people. As a coach it's essential not to make assumptions about what a coachee's values mean.

Activity: What does respect mean?

Think about the value of 'respect': what does that mean to you? Write down four words that mean 'respect' to you:

1.
2.
3.
4.

Tension brewing – Callum and his boss Jake

Callum and Jake work within the sales function of an IT company and there is tension between them. They both received coaching and worked with their coach on identifying their values. Interestingly, both of them have a core value of *respect* and yet it means something completely different for each of them:

Jake's definition: *respect* = trust, space, freedom, initiative.
Callum's definition: *respect* = support, acknowledgement, loyalty, recognition.

Callum is feeling quite stressed with his role and feels he gets no support whatsoever from his boss Jake. Meanwhile Callum feels that he shows his team respect by trusting them to get on with their jobs and giving them the space and freedom they need to get things done, without constantly looking over their shoulder.

Is it a surprise that there's some tension between Callum and Jake? Jake is behaving in a way that fits with his interpretation of 'respect' without understanding what it means to Callum. Regard for others and awareness of others would be useful here to ease the situation.

When you value other people, you take the time to understand them. When you're really tuned in to how other people feel, you can pick up when they're feeling low, stressed, etc. The thing with values is that they are deep within our emotional brain, so they need to be brought to the surface and into our awareness. Here's a sample dialogue between Jane and her EI coach:

Coach: Jane, you've said you'd like to work on your values today, to find out what really motivates you.
Jane: Yes, I'm feeling demotivated and want a change. I'm even thinking about leaving my job.

Coach: Let's start with me asking you a few questions and I'd like you to answer instinctively, with whatever comes up for you. So let's start with, 'What's really important to you in your life?'

Jane: Without doubt, my family – my husband and my children.

Coach: What does your family bring you Jane?

Jane: I love the time we spend together. I really feel I belong and the sharing is also important to me.

Coach: So, belonging and sharing are important to you?

Jane: They absolutely are. The love I feel for my family and the love I receive from them is also important to me.

Coach: What else is important to you?

Jane: Well, my career was, until recently that is. The work has changed and I'm actually quite bored with it now.

Coach: What's changed about it for you?

Jane: Well, it was more about creating new ideas and ways of working, and now it's more about administration and boring processes.

Coach: So, what did your work give you before it changed?

Jane: Lots of opportunity for creativity, but it's not there now.

Coach: What do you enjoy doing, Jane, when you're not working?

Jane: I love walking; we often go away for family weekends and go walking together. It's fantastic.

Coach: What does the walking give you?

Jane: It's a real escape for me and is all about relaxation.

Coach: If I were to ask you what gets under your skin or what annoys you, what would you say?

Jane: I can't bear intolerance of others, particularly at work or in the news. I can feel myself getting angry just speaking about it.

Coach: If intolerance makes you angry, and you were to turn that upside down, what is it that's important to you?

Jane: Fairness is hugely important to me.

Coach: So to summarize Jane, you've said that belonging, sharing, love, relaxation, creativity and fairness are important to you. Is that right?

Jane: That is absolutely right. That's me.

Activity: Define your values

It's now time for you to think about your values. What really motivates you? Table 6.1 contains a list of questions and we'd ask you to answer intuitively with what comes up for you. Even better would be to ask someone to take you through this process, so you tap into your emotional brain. For the purpose of this exercise, aim to identify six values.

Table 6.1 Values questions

1.   What is really important to you in your life?

1a. What does . . . . give you/bring you?

2.   What else is important to you in your life?

2a. What does . . . . give you/bring you?

3.   What do you enjoy doing?

3a. What does that give you/bring you?

4.   What annoys you? What gets under your skin?

4a. If xyz annoys you, if you turn that upside down, what is it that's important to you?

Once you have identified six values, put them into the left-hand column of Table 6.2. Then score how in line your life is at the moment with each value, on a scale of 1 to 10 (1 being not at all in line to 10 being in total alignment). You could use Table 6.3 to divide your values into those that are important at work and at home.

Table 6.2 Values/scoring

Value	Scoring

Table 6.3 Values at home, values at work

	At Home	At Work
Value	....	....
Value	....	....
Value	....	....

Do your values ever change?

This is a common question and opinions are often divided on the answer. We believe your core values are probably in place come late childhood, and yet your values will certainly change in priority. This can depend on a life-changing event or a different phase in your life. Other values, such as career values, may well develop over time.

VALUES AT WORK IN ORGANIZATIONS

'Values are the invisible threads between people, performance and profit' (Henderson *et al*, 2006).

Unfortunately so many companies get it completely wrong when it comes to values. How many organizations have you visited where the company values are displayed on an impressive plaque on the wall in the reception area? How many of the company employees would be able to tell you what those values are? How many of the employees who know the stated values also experience them on a day-to-day basis through the behaviour of their leaders, managers and supervisors? Unfortunately this is far too rare and the values are little more than wallpaper!

Stated or aspirational values are ok, but what matters are the real or experienced values within an organization. Traditionally, leaders have put a lot of emphasis on value and considered values as less important. With so many organizations now recognizing that people are their best asset, values give organizations a competitive and cost-effective edge when they're really used well.

Stated or real values?

Consider these values and the type of organization they might belong to:

- communication;
- respect;
- integrity;
- excellence.

What do you think of these values? Pretty impressive, by anyone's standards. This is the set of values that were displayed in a very famous (or rather infamous) organization – Enron! Clearly there was a big difference between its stated values and the actual culture, attitudes and behaviours.

When you are thinking about your organization's values, assess which of these three levels they are currently at:

- Stated values (they've been defined and communicated, verbally, or in writing, or both).
- Lived/experienced values (the leaders of the business live the values, employees know and experience the values through the behaviours of their leaders, and coachees benefit from and understand what the values are).
- Applied and aligned values (they're alive and well in the organization and form an active role in the business, used as part of the decision-making process, for defining acceptable behaviours, to resolve conflict situations, etc).

It is not enough for values just to be stated: they need to be at the very least understood by everyone in the business and lived by the leaders (in terms of how they behave on a daily basis). Actions definitely speak louder than values! We will look at how to set company values that work later in this chapter.

ATTITUDES AND BELIEFS

Attitudes and beliefs can help individuals and organizations move forward and achieve their goals, or not as the case may be. EI coaching helps individuals, teams and organizations identify and change the limiting attitudes and beliefs that stop full potential being achieved. While values determine what motivates and drives you, your beliefs and attitudes will also strongly impact your behaviour and the results you achieve (or not as the case may be). Figure 6.2 shows the relationship between performance and satisfaction; try this for yourself, using the grid in Figure 6.3.

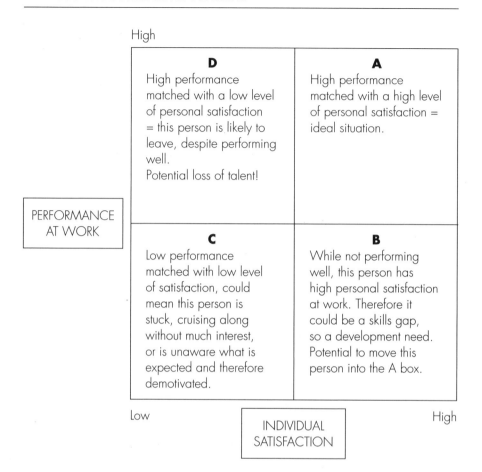

High

D	**A**
High performance matched with a low level of personal satisfaction = this person is likely to leave, despite performing well. Potential loss of talent!	High performance matched with a high level of personal satisfaction = ideal situation.
C	**B**
Low performance matched with low level of satisfaction, could mean this person is stuck, cruising along without much interest, or is unaware what is expected and therefore demotivated.	While not performing well, this person has high personal satisfaction at work. Therefore it could be a skills gap, so a development need. Potential to move this person into the A box.

PERFORMANCE AT WORK

Low

High

INDIVIDUAL SATISFACTION

Figure 6.2   Performance at work vs individual satisfaction

Angela and the career change

Angela decided to work with a coach as she felt she was at a crossroads in her career. She'd worked in an engineering company for several years and she was bored with the work she was doing. She was working in an administrative type of job, so spent a lot of time using the computer. Through doing a values exercise she realized why she was bored: creativity and caring were two of her core values. Using her logical thinking brain, she knew that the best option would be to move companies and yet something was holding her back. When the coach asked her some challenging questions about what was getting in the way, she said 'I'm too old to change jobs.'

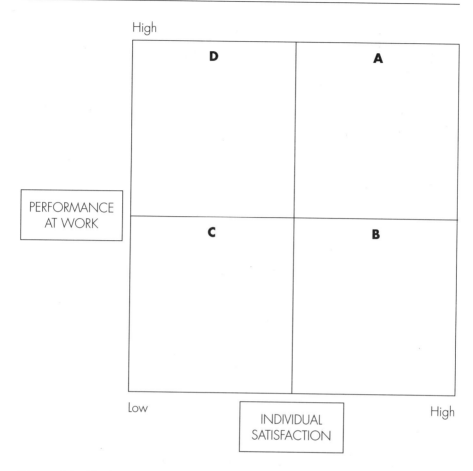

Figure 6.3   Performance at work vs individual satisfaction grid

A limiting belief had surfaced, and was definitely getting in the way of Angela taking any action. Any ideas how old she was? Just 30! Angela believed this to be the absolute truth and so the coach asked her who she knew who'd changed jobs and even industries after the age of 30. To start with, Angela couldn't think of anyone, but she decided to think about it in between coaching sessions. A week later, Angela came back with a list of 10 people she knew who'd changed jobs beyond the age of 30. This blew her belief out of the water that people didn't change jobs after 30, and she started to take positive action to move herself closer to what really motivated her.

Activity: Give your beliefs and attitudes a spring clean!

It's important to remember that beliefs and attitudes live in our emotional brain and we often don't even know they're there. Think about how you'd complete these statements and answer with the first thing that comes up for you:

I am _____.
My work is _____.
Life is _____.
Money is _____.
Age is _____.
People are _____.

Is what you wrote down positive, negative or even quite neutral?

Successful people have positive inspiring beliefs and attitudes that help them achieve great things. What kind of things do you think someone like Bill Gates or Richard Branson believes? 'Anything's possible', 'I can do anything I put my mind to' might be some examples. Are your beliefs and attitudes helping you achieve your greatness? If they're not, the good news is that you can change them, with the help of your logical thinking brain.

Activity: Addressing negative beliefs and attitudes at work

Your task here is to listen. For the next five days at work, listen to what people around you are saying and make a note of them. Also, what do you notice about their whole being and feelings? Do you hear any negative attitudes and beliefs? Listen out for things like:

That always happens to me.
I can't do that.
I'll never get that contract/promotion/bonus.
It won't work.

Watch out for negative energy and emotions too.

Remember that most of these attitudes/beliefs live in your colleagues' unconscious brains and they may not be aware of them. You can support them in an emotionally intelligent way (maintaining your own self-regard and having a high regard for others), by reflecting things back to them or asking them questions about it. For example:

Sally: I don't know why I'm even going for that promotion. I'll never get it. I never get the jobs I want.
June: Never? Have you ever got a job you wanted?
Sally: Well, I suppose so. I got this job three years ago, but I bet I won't get this one.
June: What could you be saying to yourself that would be more supportive?
Sally: Not sure really. I suppose I could tell myself that I've got as good a chance as anyone else.
June: That sounds good. Why not give it a go?

THE VALUES, ATTITUDES AND BEHAVIOUR LINK

As we explained in Chapter 1, your values, beliefs, attitudes, thoughts and feelings are all interconnected and they impact on your behaviour and actions on a daily basis. With repetition you form habits. Take stock of your day-to-day actions, reactions, responses and behaviours for the next week. What are the values that are driving your behaviour and are your beliefs and attitudes really supporting you to be the best you can be?

As a coach, your values, beliefs and attitudes will have an impact on the kinds of questions you ask your coachee, in the same way that coachees' values, beliefs and attitudes will affect how they answer, how they interpret an event and ultimately what action (if any) they take. As Dr Patrick Williams says: 'Coaching at its best can help coachees shift limiting attitudes and beliefs and help them really think outside the box.'

Values and attitudes in an emotional intelligence context

Your values and attitudes live in your emotional brain and are a very powerful force in your life. They affect your behaviours, which ultimately impact your results and performance in life. Understanding and respecting your own and others' values is important for self-regard and regard for others. By maintaining a high self-awareness, you'll immediately know if your values are being stepped on and you can use your self-management to bring them back into line. Being aware of others, you'll also be able to tell if you step on others' values and, using your relationship management skills, you can put the situation right.

The emotionally intelligent coach (EI coach)

Emotionally intelligent coaches are highly aware of their own values and mindful of their own beliefs and attitudes, which can have an impact on the coaching process. Their values, beliefs and attitudes will undoubtedly influence the questions they ask and their emotional and logical responses to what the coachee says.

The emotionally intelligent organization

The emotionally intelligent organization will recognize that every single one of its employees has a unique set of values, beliefs and attitudes. When recruiting new staff, it will ensure values fit and recruit for the right attitudes (people's skills can be trained more easily than their attitudes can be changed). It will also have an organizational set of values that are real and lived by its leaders and team members. They will be aligned with a set of positive attitudes and behaviours that are understood by everyone. People know what's expected of them and how their job roles fit in with the values of the organization.

Let's take the example of an engineering company that went through a process of identifying its organizational values. It involved its key decision makers and a cross-section of its employees in defining its core values, with respect being the number one value. As we suggested earlier in this chapter, it broke it down in the following way so everyone understood what it meant and what was expected of them:

Value: Respect
Attitude: We respect ourselves, our colleagues and our customers at all times.
Behaviours: We keep our word and do what we say we're going to do. If for any reason we cannot keep to commitments, we'll tell you immediately.

It uses its values when it sets organizational objectives and when it makes decisions, so they're completely aligned and working with everyone's best interests in mind.

DEFINING ORGANIZATIONAL VALUES, ATTITUDES AND BEHAVIOURS

The following five steps can be used as a basic outline for defining and implementing values in an organizational setting that are real, understood and lived by everyone:

Step 1. Define the values (up to a maximum of five) – through facilitated sessions with the team who set the organizational strategy, and if possible focus groups of a cross-section of employees.
Step 2. Describe what these values actually mean. Interpretation is very important.
Step 3. Identify the attitudes you expect to be adopted in line with these values, which apply to everyone.
Step 4. Define the behaviours that link in to these values and attitudes. It is important to make an extensive list of behaviours connected to each value, otherwise people will not live the company value. (How can they be expected to live it if they don't even know what it means?)
Step 5. Communicate these behaviours through team briefings and be creative in how you use them: you could have them printed on cards and given to everyone. Ensure they're in every office, in company literature, etc.

It is also important to ensure the values are being lived and experienced. Leaders need to 'walk the talk' otherwise the values will be meaningless. You could check at monthly or quarterly meetings how you are living the organizational values, use them as a benchmark to recruit, and ensure they're visible and being used. If organizations have them, it's essential they live them!

Summary

- When you know your values and you have a positive set of beliefs and attitudes and work within an organization that does the same, this really leads to performance without effort.
- Emotionally intelligent coaching can help you achieve a clear understanding of your values and how you can live them.
- Your values are what motivate you: they're your own internal compass.
- Values help you better understand yourself and other people.
- You can use values as a great decision-making tool.

■ Organizational values must be real (not just stated or aspirational) and experienced by employees and customers alike.

■ Values-driven organizations have competitive advantage, if they're really true to those values.

■ Recruit for values, beliefs and attitudes, and train for skills (most companies recruit on skills and experience alone).

■ Negative beliefs and attitudes hold you back and cost you dearly.

■ Your values, beliefs and attitudes *do* affect your performance.

■ Emotionally intelligent coaches know their own values, have positive beliefs and attitudes and are aware of how they impact the coaching process.

■ The emotionally intelligent organization has a clearly defined set of values that are lived and breathed by their employees and experienced by their customers. Individuals' values are also respected.

References

Blanchard, K and O'Connor, M (2003) *Managing by Values*, Berrett-Koehler, California

Covey, S R (1999) *The 7 Habits of Highly Effective People*, Simon and Schuster, London

Drucker, P F (2007) *The Essential Drucker*, Elsevier, Oxford

Henderson, M, Thompson, D and Henderson, S (2006) *Leading through Values*, HarperCollins, London

Maslow, A (1954) *Motivation and Personality*, HarperCollins, London

Massey, M (1979) *The People Puzzle*, Reston Publishing, Reston, VA

Pearce, T (2003) *Leading Out Loud*, Jossey-Bass, San Francisco, CA

Smith, H (2001) *What Matters Most*, Simon and Schuster, London

Sparrow, T and Knight, A (2006) *Applied EI*, Wiley, Chichester

7

Core coaching skills

> *Knowledge is like climbing a mountain; the higher you reach, the more you can see and appreciate.*
>
> Anonymous

Coaching is about communication; emotional intelligence is about communication – communication with ourselves and with others. When we talk about core coaching skills, we talk about the skills we use to hear others, to talk to others and to help our coachees to articulate their thoughts, feelings and experiences. They are the skills we use unconsciously in everyday life raised to a higher level by conscious practising and development.

The ability to communicate well starts with a high level of self-regard. If we have faith in ourselves, if we believe we are worth listening to and talking to, then we are more likely to be able to listen and talk to others confidently and with great integrity. Some of the activities in Chapter 5 will help to develop your communication skills, as well as build your self-regard, regard for others, self-awareness and awareness of others.

The four pillars of EI coaching skills are:

1. Listening.
2. Questioning.
3. Empathy.
4. Rapport.

Understanding how we can use our own levels of emotional intelligence to develop these skills, and how we can use these skills to develop our emotional intelligence, is a two-way street.

DO YOU HEAR WHAT I HEAR?

How often do you come away from a conversation where you've been talking about something only to feel frustrated and irritated because you feel the other people simply have not been listening? They may have turned the conversation around to a subject they want to talk about, or only asked you questions in order to turn the topic back to them.

Too often the time when a person is 'listening' is simply the time when the other person is talking, and the 'listener' is thinking what he or she can say next! What buttons does this press for you? It can feel disrespectful, impolite, even rude, and can affect us so much that we shut up and walk away. It can even affect our relationships.

Being listened to, really listened to, is a great experience. As Nancy Kline (1999) says: 'The quality of your attention determines other people's thinking.' Listening to ourselves, our coachees and everyone with whom we have contact gives them time to think, time to reflect, and time to let their emotional brain work its magic.

How does the EI coach's listening differ then from general conversational listening and even some trained coaches' listening? Emotionally intelligent coaches use whole-body listening. They listen with eyes, body and intuition as well as their ears, and they are aware of the impact their listening has on their own emotions. General conversational listening is just what the name suggests: general and, you could say, automatic. The EI coach develops listening skills, but with the awareness that our attitude has a massive impact on how we listen. You can see from the listening spectrum in Figure 7.1 how the listener's focus shifts from the listener to the speaker.

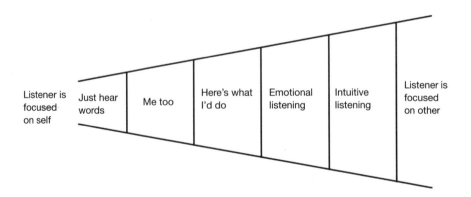

Figure 7.1   The listening spectrum

'I just hear words' listening

There are conversations where we hear words, but we don't take them in. We have so much else going on in our minds that we can be looking at a person as he or she speaks to us, but we just hear words and nothing behind them. Nothing engages with us. It's almost non-listening, except we're in the conversation. We're likely to respond with something that bears no relation to what the other person has said to us.

'Me too' listening

We've probably all had times when we're thinking about how the conversation relates to us. We think of what experiences we have to match, and ultimately we either consciously or unconsciously want to bring the conversation back to us.

'Here's what I'd do' listening

Now we're beginning to give the other person some attention. We might respond to what he or she is saying by offering information or advice. We hear what he or she asks us, and respond in an 'automatic' fashion. We're becoming more aware of his or her needs, rather than just addressing our own, even on an unconscious level.

Emotional listening

Here is where the big shift comes in the levels of listening and this is where EI coaches come into their own. The listener begins to give real space and time to the speaker, encouraging him or her to expand his or her thinking and exploration. They keep themselves out of the thought process and the focus is on the speaker and the speaker's thoughts *and* feelings. We can start to listen beyond the words, but still take care not to make any assumptions about what emotions the speaker might be experiencing. What changes are there in the speaker's tone of voice; does he or she hesitate, sigh or pause? What about his or her body language, eye contact and facial expressions?

Intuitive listening

When we're in tune with our emotional brain, and when we're truly listening at a deep level, we are listening with our entire bodies, not just our ears. We engage our intuition and the focus is entirely on the speaker. It becomes effortless to listen. Trying to listen in this way takes skill and practice, trusting our intuition and picking up other signals to make it more natural. This listening really does happen at an unconscious level, but we can develop the skills at a conscious level to help us achieve it.

Have you ever walked into a room and got a sense of what was going on through the energy and feel of the atmosphere? That is whole-body listening! When we're listening with our entire bodies and intuition, it's important that we keep any judgement out of the equation, otherwise intuition can fall into assumption. If we put our own interpretation on the situation, based on our intuition, then we begin to see the challenge or situation from our own perspective. We begin to make assumptions about the way the other person thinks and feels. If we look at the following example dialogue, we can see how easy it is to pick up on something using our intuition, but then put our own interpretation on it, and get it very wrong:

A: I'd like to go for the promotion, but I don't think I'd be able to cope with the hours it would require.
B: I'm sensing you're feeling you're not good enough for this job.
A: Do you? Why? No, it's not that, I'm concerned about the travelling. I'd be great in the job, but I don't want to be away from home as much as it would demand.

B was picking up on some hesitancy or other signs that A didn't feel totally comfortable; however, B attached some of his or her own anxieties or discomfort about job changes to the situation and made a huge assumption. Keeping it non-directive and neutral allows the coachee or the other person to explore just what it is that is underneath the non-verbal communication.

So how do the levels of listening we've explored here link with EI? Two key scales of emotional intelligence linked directly to effective listening are self-awareness and awareness of others. Remember, our self-awareness is about being in touch with how we feel and recognizing what's going on in our body that acts as an emotional barometer. Our awareness of others helps us pick up on signals that others are giving, helping us be aware that other things may be going on for them. We need to keep our judgement out of labelling what that might be. Again, intuition can easily become an assumption if we don't use our awareness of others accurately.

Being self-aware when we listen

When we're getting ready for a coaching session we clear a space to be ready to listen to whatever our coachees want to talk to us about. We put our focus on to them and there is no place for our 'stuff' when we're coaching. When we are self-aware we'll know what that 'stuff' is, or at least the impact it's having on us. We can check how we're feeling going into the session, what our thoughts are, and use techniques to put our own thoughts to one side so as to concentrate on our coachee.

When we can acknowledge our own feelings and thoughts before we coach, we can reflect on them and learn more about ourselves. It's also important to remember, though, that we are human! That means that our coachee's emotions, feelings and thoughts can also affect us. Being resilient and aware will help us keep it in perspective.

The powerful role of intuition

'Intuition is what your brain knows how to do when you leave it alone', according to Dr Paul MacLean (1990), former Chief of Brain Evolution, US National Institute of Mental Health.

How often have you said, 'I should have trusted my intuition'? Trusting our intuition depends on our emotional intelligence, and the great thing is that it can be developed. Self-awareness is the key to that development. If we pay attention to our bodies and listen to our own thoughts and begin to make sense of them, we can improve our intuitive skills.

When you're thinking about something, you're using your logical brain, using your cognitive powers, and it serves you well. Once you've done that, practise pausing. Check with the rest of your body: what is your gut feeling? Remember that 6 billion nerve cells are firing in the emotional brain compared to the 100 of the logical brain. If you let your emotional brain tell you something, what would it say?

Coaches can use their intuition to connect to the coachee's meaning (intuitive listening) and to stimulate the coachee's own intuition (self-awareness), but also to share intuitive data between the two (intuitive learning).

Activity: intuition

Try this exercise right now. Bring something to mind that you're pondering or considering at the moment, maybe a decision you need to make.

Think about it from different perspectives, alternative solutions, what other people might suggest if you asked them. What would be a logical solution?

Now pause. Listen to your body. What is it saying? You may not notice anything. Relax and pause again. Where are you feeling any tension or excitement; do you have any physical sensations? Become aware of your body language. Are you relaxed? Are you tense? What feeling are you experiencing?

It may take a while until anything comes to you, but it's worth practising. You'll begin to notice a sense whether the solution you've come to 'feels right' or not. That's intuition kicking in.

What else is your intuition telling you about this decision?

Working with both your logical and emotional brains gives a rounded perspective. So when we're listening to a coachee, listening to what our bodies and emotional brain are telling us raises the game of our listening skills. Intuition is described in dictionaries as the 'instinctive knowledge of or belief about something without conscious reasoning'. We know the lion is more powerful than the lion tamer, so why not work with it rather than ignoring its presence?

EI LISTENING

EI listening is whole-body, intuitive, non-judgemental listening. To develop your EI listening, try doing the following exercise with a partner.

Activity: EI listening

Give yourselves time and space to really focus on the practice of listening with your whole body. Notice what happens to your ability to pick up on what's going on for you, and what's going on for your partner.

One of you talk for three to five minutes on any topic that interests you which you can speak about uninterrupted for that length of time. The listener only makes encouraging noises, asks no questions, doesn't interrupt and demonstrates positive body language (we will look further at rapport later in this chapter).

As the listener, keep your focus on the speaker. What do you pick up from the language they use? What do you notice about the tone and pitch of their voice? What do you pick up from their body language? How do they sit? What is their eye contact like? Let your unconscious mind absorb what's going on; don't try to put logical thought around it. You are not coaching, you don't need to ask questions. You are simply giving your partner the respect of listening while they speak.

When the speaker has finished speaking, before you offer any feedback on how it was to listen, pause and become aware of how you felt when you were listening. Did you feel relaxed? Did you experience anything that triggered some distraction that took you away from listening? What is your intuition telling you, if anything? What did you experience in your body and where?

Tell the other person what it was like to listen. If you sensed something in your intuition then reflect it back, keeping assumptions out, rather than asking whether your intuition might have been accurate.

After you switch roles and you now speak for three to five minutes, reflect on what it was like to be totally listened to for that length of time, and to have someone else's undivided attention. What did you experience during that time? It may feel uncomfortable as it is unusual to have that uninterrupted opportunity. How did it feel? When we coach we use silence as a means of giving space and time to consider and reflect. Experience its power in this exercise.

Empathic listening

Empathic or active listening is more than just listening. It involves giving clues back to the person we're listening to that we understand what he or she is talking about. We're putting ourselves in his or her shoes, as much as we can.

Thinking again about the difference between intuition and assumption, it's important when we reflect back what we've heard to our coachees that we keep our own judgement and perspective out of it. Intuition is what we experience when we listen to our emotional brain. Assumption is what we experience when our logical brain gets involved and misinterprets the signals from our emotional brain!

> So when you are listening to somebody, completely, attentively, then you are listening not only to the words, but also to the feeling of what is being conveyed, to the whole of it, not part of it. (Jiddu Krishnamurti, 1997)

Tim Sparrow suggests there are five elements for empathic listening and they support our views on the EI coach's listening skills. These elements are:

1. Empty yourself: be with the other person. This means that we manage our own 'stuff' while we're listening. We talked about this earlier in the chapter.
2. Give attention: focus on what we're hearing, feeling and experiencing.
3. Give acceptance: accept the person we're listening to for who he or she is.
4. Make no judgement or comparison: we may acknowledge how what we're hearing matches or clashes with our values and beliefs, but we don't judge.
5. Stay with the feeling: learn to love your intuition.

What gets in the way of being able to listen effectively, with our whole bodies, not just our ears? There are basically three things that get in the way: what we're thinking, what we're feeling and what we're doing.

If we have thoughts running in our mind, we can't focus on the speaker. If we're having an emotional response to what's being said, it can distract us from listening well. If we're distracted, we might end up displaying body language that shows we're distracted. We might look away, we might interrupt inappropriately, or we might start to lead or direct the conversation.

If you complete the listening activity in Chapter 5, you will be more aware of what might get in the way of your being able to listen really effectively.

Silence is golden

When we're comfortable and practised at listening with our whole bodies, we can sit with silence in the coaching session. How rarely do we have silence in our everyday conversations? Often people like to fill the silence as they feel uncomfortable and awkward. Silence is mistaken for a sign that the other person has nothing to say, doesn't want to talk to you or is waiting for you to speak.

Silence in the coaching session creates a wonderful environment in which to think! When we're listening, we can be comfortable with silence. It's the part where the coachee thinks without confusion, thinks without interruption, where he or she finds solutions.

EMOTIONALLY INTELLIGENT QUESTIONING

If the quality of our attention is one thing that impacts on other people's thinking, then making sure our questions relate to what we're hearing demonstrates our attention. If we listen at the highest level and ask questions that are open and non-judgemental, the other person's thinking will have the greatest chance of being outstanding.

When our levels of self-regard and regard for others are high, our questions are more likely to be respectful, non-judgemental and solution-seeking. The only reason a coach asks questions of the coachee in the coaching session is for the coachee's benefit, to release thinking.

You may be familiar with open and closed questions and they both have a place in the coaching dialogue. Open questions are an invitation to explore, consider options and to find solutions eg, 'What impact does that have on you?' Closed questions elicit yes or no answers, or gather information for the benefit of both coach and coachee eg, 'Is that having an impact on you?'

In Chapter 5 we looked at other sorts of questions: follow-on questions eg, 'Tell me more about that.' 'What else is important there?' Coaching isn't a chat, it's a conversation, a dialogue that is intended to make a difference to the coachee. So we need to probe, go beyond the 'first answer': 'What else might you not have thought of yet?' And there are evaluative questions: 'How might that affect you? How does it match with your values?'

Health warning: questions to avoid!

If we let our judgement cloud a question, we can end up asking leading or judgemental questions. We could even hide a solution we think might work in a question eg, 'How could you set up a meeting with your boss to get this dispute sorted?'

'Why' questions can sometimes be interpreted as judgemental or aggressive and the response from the coachee can be defensive, almost justifying his or her thoughts, feelings or ideas eg, 'Why haven't you completed the actions from last time?'

Occasionally we fall into the trap of asking more complicated questions than needed. Simple questions often have a greater impact on the emotional brain than long, complicated ones. This can happen when the coach is trying to get to an answer he or she feels is the right one. Trust the coachees can find their own.

Sometimes people ask multiple questions, two or three questions in one sentence. How confusing is that for the coachee, not knowing which one to answer first? Powerful questions need space around them to work best eg, 'What could you have done differently and how and when would you have done it?'

QUESTIONING AND THE EI COACH

The EI coach asks questions that tap into the coachee's emotional brain. They are questions that help the coachee recognize and acknowledge his or her feelings, questions that explore the coachee's self-awareness and encourage reflective learning. The EI coach may also ask questions about the elements of emotional intelligence that will support the coachee's own EI development.

Questions that encourage wisdom in the coachee are those that coaches ask when they are listening to their own intuition. When coaches have high levels of self-awareness and awareness of others and when they are coming from the healthiest life position of 'I'm ok, you're ok', there is the greatest chance that they will ask the most effective questions.

Activity: Powerful questions

Look at the following questions and identify those that hit the spot for you! Which have a positive powerful impact on your emotional brain?

1. What is going on for you right now?
2. What do you really want?
3. What does that feel like?
4. Where do you feel it?
5. Who's the real you?
6. How does today fit in with your forever plans?
7. How will you live your magnificence?
8. What else could I ask?
9. How will you know when you're living your dream?
10. What gets in the way?

Rate each question on a scale of 1 to 10 in terms of the positive impact it has on you, where 1 is not much of an impact and 10 is *wow*!

What gives those questions such a positive impact? They are short, non-directive and encourage the listener to think deeply.

To raise our own level of communication skills we regularly reflect on the impact of the questions we ask our coachees. It's good practice for coaches to reflect on each coaching session immediately afterwards. If we tap into our awareness of others we will recognize those questions that connect with our coachee, and those that have less impact.

How do we know when we've asked the question that unsticks our coachees? Often it's when they go silent. If they do go silent, stay with it. There's nothing quite as powerful as sitting with your coachees as they let their thoughts develop and crystallize. It demonstrates great awareness of others to maintain the silence with them.

EI EMPATHY

Empathy is the building block for positive relationships. It is about acknowledging how others feel and imagining being in their shoes but without judgement. Daniel Goleman (2005) calls empathy our 'social radar'. People lacking in empathy find it difficult to relate to others. You sometimes hear people saying to each other, 'I know exactly how you feel'? It's impossible to know *exactly* how someone else feels. Their feelings are connected to their experiences, their attitudes and their values and are unique to them. We can certainly say we can imagine how we'd feel if we were in their shoes. Is it helpful for a coach to show empathy in this way?

In Chapter 3 we read the story of little Ben and how his father showed a total lack of empathy due to low awareness of others. Putting empathy into a coaching context we can see how our self-awareness and awareness of others supports an empathic perspective:

Coachee: It just feels impossible. I never expected to be made redundant at this age. I can't begin to see how I can get another job now.

Coach: I can hear this is difficult for you. What do you feel right now about the situation?

Coachee: I feel lost, scared and that I've let everyone down.

Coach: What does it look like from your perspective?

The coach is staying with the coachee while he or she expresses how he or she feels about the situation. By staying with the coachee, the coach demonstrates that he or she is listening, almost asking for help to understand what it's like for the coachee without putting any of his or her own perspective on it.

Notice what it's like when others try to imagine what it's like for you, and notice what it's like when they make assumptions about how you must be feeling. It's a very powerful difference! Have you ever been miles away in your mind, in a complete daydream about something? You might be thinking about what's going to be happening that evening; you might be planning your holiday details. You might be simply making a mental food shopping list! Then someone sees you and says, 'Cheer up, it might never happen.' This doesn't make any sense to you! You weren't unhappy, or scared, or sad; you were simply thinking. They'd seen your expression (deep thought) and interpreted it as sadness. How wrong could they be!

RAPPORT

In Chapter 5 we heard about how we can listen with our eyes, not just our ears and that has been explored in the listening section of this chapter. Listening with our eyes as well as our ears, and our whole bodies, is what helps us build rapport with others. Rapport is the connection we make when we are aware of others, have high regard for others as well as for ourselves, and are genuine in the way we communicate with others. Genuine rapport builds relationships with others.

How do you know when rapport is good? Have you ever noticed how when you're really enjoying a conversation with someone you start to mirror each other's body language and mannerisms? You might find you're both crossing your legs or arms in a similar way, either mirroring or matching the other person. You might find you tip your head if he or she does, or match his or her speed of talking. If you do mirror or match naturally, then your rapport will build and will be genuine. If you deliberately mirror or match without having high regard for the other person, the chances are that he or she will sense something's not right, and it could actually have a detrimental effect on the rapport between you.

In his book, *Social Intelligence,* Daniel Goleman (2007) describes mirror neurones as nerve cells in our emotional brain that help us pick up on what others are feeling and start mirroring their behaviours, without being aware of it at a conscious level at all. We can't force these to work; they operate on an unconscious level. However, if we have genuinely high regard for others, there is a greater chance they will start working when we are in conversations with others. We can also develop our awareness of how these mirror neurones are used between others. Next time you are at a social gathering, notice how people unconsciously match each other's body language. Or why not try this? Say there's a group of you talking together, and you find the speaker seems to be speaking directly to you and not looking at others in the group, even though the whole group is involved in the conversation. If you break eye contact with the speaker and look at another member of the group, the speaker is almost certainly going to follow your eyes, and look at the person you've just looked at. Why? Because their mirror neurones are doing their job!

There are ways of developing your rapport-building skills in an emotionally intelligent and authentic way. Notice when your conversations flow with family, friends, work colleagues and strangers. What's happening when you meet someone for the first time and you come away from the encounter thinking, 'He was easy to talk to' or, 'I feel like I've known her for ages!'

Be aware of your body language. Do you find yourself mirroring in a natural way? Use your self-awareness to learn what works and what happens. What's happening when you feel uncomfortable in someone's presence? Is rapport good? If not, what's happening? Being able to make your coachee feel comfortable and able to trust you is the starting point of a great coaching relationship.

A note about phone rapport

One of the questions we are often asked as coaches is, when coaching on the telephone, is it still possible to build good rapport even though you can't see the other person? The answer is yes; you can still match and mirror tone of voice and speed of talking. If rapport is good you might even mirror body language, even though you can't see each other!

The three Is

Have you ever been in a conversation where you say something that is very clear to you and the other person reacts in a way that takes you totally by surprise? Or have you ever done something pretty much unconsciously and someone else has totally misinterpreted it?

The three Is are intention, interpretation and impact, and they are linked with each other inextricably. Imagine you're attending a networking event, and are looking forward to meeting Michael with whom you hope to do business. You walk into the room, see Michael talking to someone else in a group, and decide to leave it until he's free. In the meantime, Michael caught sight of you looking across at him, and then noticed you didn't come over to talk to him. This surprised him as you'd arranged to meet there. He assumes you have changed your mind and didn't want to talk business with him. He turns back to the group and decides that it'll be up to you to come find him, and if you don't, then he won't do business with you. Your intention was to leave Michael alone until he was free to talk; his interpretation was that you didn't want to talk; and the impact was that he felt slightly negative towards the idea of doing business with you.

When someone behaves in a way you're not expecting, is that because he or she interpreted your behaviour in a different way to which it was intended? What impact might that have in a coaching scenario?

COACHING MODELS

There are many coaching models used by coaches. The purpose is to create a structure, or framework, for the coach to keep the session on track, to give the coachee a sense of structure. They are the bean poles in your vegetable garden. They help the bean plants grow tall and straight, leaving enough light between the plants for the sunshine to reach the beans. The poles don't restrict the beans as they grow – they support them.

Coaches in training may find it helpful to consider what questions they could ask about each element, not to pre-empt any discussions they may have with their coachee, but to support learning and development away from the coaching session. In Chapter 9 you will find other models, such as the PAUSE model and the Goal Flow Map. The purpose of both of those is similar: to provide a framework for the coach.

The EI COACH model encompasses both the process of coaching and the principles of EI. It builds a framework for the coach to check the coachee's feelings at the beginning and end of the session. It also explores the current situation and where the coachee would like to be, and focuses on actions and behaviours that are necessary to effect change.

The EI COACH model

E = Emotions (How are you feeling?)
I = Intelligence (What do you want to talk about and achieve today?)
C = Current (What's going on for you right now?)
O = Opportunities (What possibilities are available to you?)
A = Actions (What are you going to do?)
C = Change measure (What difference will this make? How will you know you're there?)
H = How are you feeling now? (Emotional barometer.)

Let's take a closer look at the EI COACH model. What questions might come into each element? How does the model support the EI development of the participants as well as support outstanding coaching?

Emotions

At the outset of the session, the EI coach checks in with the coachee as to how he or she is feeling. The benefit of this when it happens on a regular basis is that the coachee begins to build his or her own self-awareness. The coachee begins to develop his or her own emotional barometer both in and outside of the coaching session.

- How are you feeling today?
- Where do you feel it?
- What does it tell you?

Intelligence

- What's the session about?
- Where would be a great place to be at the end of the session?
- What internal resources do you have that will help you get there?

Current

- What's going on for you right now regarding this issue?
- What challenges do you face?

- What's working really well for you?
- What strengths will help you?
- What's the truth of the situation?
- What assumptions might you be making?
- What do you believe about the situation?
- How much does that help or hinder you?

Opportunities

- What options are open to you?
- What could you do?
- How would that fit in with who you are?
- How would it help you reach your goal?
- What feels right about them?
- Which ones take you nearer to your values?
- Which ones might take you further away from your values?
- What's great about your ideas?

Action

- What are you going to do?
- What will you commit to?
- How will you make it happen?
- What else do you need to be able to achieve it?
- What's your timeline for this?
- Who else would it be useful to involve?
- How do you feel about the actions you've chosen?
- How do you think it will go?

Change measure

- How will you know when you've achieved what you want to?
- What difference will it make?
- What will you experience, see and hear?

How do you feel now?

- What's worked well for you today?
- What are you feeling?

Whatever your coaching role, whether professional coach, manager or leader, the EI COACH model supports your emotional intelligence and that of your coachee and your team.

Summary

■ Listening, questioning, empathy and rapport form the four pillars of EI coaching skills.

■ The EI coach is able to listen without judgement, question without needing to know the answer, and can show empathy and build rapport.

■ The EI COACH model offers a framework for emotionally intelligent coaching.

■ Listening crosses a spectrum from where the listener's focus is on themselves to where the listener's focus is on the speaker.

■ The five levels of listening are:
  – 'I just hear words' listening;
  – 'Me too' listening;
  – 'Here's what I'd do' listening;
  – emotional listening;
  – intuitive listening.

■ We listen with our whole bodies, not just our ears.

■ Check our self-awareness when we listen – feel what's happening for us.

■ Empathy is about imagining ourselves in the other person's shoes, as much as we can.

■ Intuition is what your brain does when you leave it alone.

■ Assumption is what happens when you put your own spin on your intuition.

■ Silence is golden! It creates a space for the other person to think.

■ Make sure the questions you ask are for the benefit of the coachee, rather than for you.

■ Rapport is the connection we make when we are aware of others, have high regard for others as well as for ourselves and are genuine in the way we communicate with others.

■ All communication has three elements to consider: intention, interpretation and impact (the three Is).

References

Gladwell, M (2005) *Blink,* Penguin, Harmondsworth

Goleman, D (2005) *Emotional Intelligence: Why it can matter more than IQ,* Bantam, New York

Goleman, D (2007) *Social Intelligence: The new science of human relationships,* Arrow Books, London

Kline, N (1999) *Time to Think,* Cassell Illustrated, London

Krishnamurti, J (1997) *Freedom from the Known,* Harper, San Francisco, CA

MacLean, P (1990) *The Triune Brain in Evolution,* Plenum Press, New York

Sparrow, T and Knight, A (2006) *Applied EI,* Wiley, Chichester

8

How goals flow from values to action

> *Goals help focus you on areas in both your personal and professional life that are important and meaningful, rather than being guided by what other people want you to be, do, or accomplish.*
>
> Catherine Pulsifer

If our values represent our highest priorities, doesn't it make absolute sense that our goals and dreams are rooted in our values? Yet how often do we pursue things, jobs, careers, relationships, even possessions, and when we achieve what we think we desired, we feel let down, somehow dissatisfied and disappointed?

We've seen how our values form the internal blueprint that makes us who we are and how they are linked intrinsically with our attitudes and self-regard. If our values are so completely linked with our identity, how can it make any sense at all if we don't set our goals in line with our fundamental being? And yet we do. We do it as individuals and we do it as organizations. We set New Year's resolutions that have fallen by the wayside by the time Easter comes around. According to an article in the *Daily Telegraph* in January 2007, January is the most popular month for joining a gym, with almost 12 per cent of memberships taken out. But the Fitness Industry Association said that almost 22 per cent of people who join will have thrown in the towel after 24 weeks. A further 20 per cent will disappear before December. Why? Because we're either doing it for the wrong reason, or we don't know why we're doing it. As we saw in Chapter 6, if your goals don't reflect your values, it will be hard work to stick to them.

Organizations set targets in their business and strategic plans. How often are those goals and targets aligned with the organization's values? Values are 'the invisible threads between people, performance and profit'. They have so much more potency when they are integral to the vision and strategy of the organization.

So, in this chapter we are going to explore:

■ How to set dynamic, values-driven goals.
■ How to engage our emotional intelligence when establishing and working towards our goals.
■ How to use our strengths to make sure we achieve what we set out to achieve.
■ How to be aware when the goals we've set simply aren't congruent with our identity, are disappointing to us, or just don't get us to where we'd like to be.

Remember the analogy of the ladder being up against the wrong wall? This chapter and the activities in it will help you make sure your ladder is up against the best wall for you and you'll know why!

EVERYTHING STARTS AS AN IDEA

What are goals?

Goals are either what we want to be, what we want to do or what we want to have, which at this moment we are not being, are not doing, or do not have. For example:

■ *Be.* We may want to be promoted, we may want to be fitter, we may want to be in a relationship.
■ *Do.* We might aspire to run a marathon, learn to fly or beat a personal best.
■ *Have.* Having a new house, a once-in-a-lifetime holiday. We might set our sights on having a new job or building a more engaged team.

Activity: Your goals

What goals do you have right now that would fit into one of these categories? Make a note here of what they are, and which sort of goal they are:

Be   **Do**   **Have**

How much of that list is something you're working towards every day? How much of that list is new, simply because you're now thinking about it? How much of the list surprises you?

As well as realizing that goals are what we want to be, do or have, it's helpful to know what sort of goal it is:

- *Go up goals.* John has a desire to learn to fly. It's something that's fascinated and attracted him since his teens. He wants to be able to fly as a hobby but also sees it as a possible career change in the future. This is a go up goal for something he wants to achieve.
- *Give up goals.* Sarah wants to cut down on her alcohol intake as it's become a bit of a habit and she decides on a plan to drink only at weekends for three months to see what difference it makes. This is her give up goal to feel healthier.
- *Deficit goals.* Phil has been told by his doctor that he needs to cut back on the running as it's damaging his knee cartilage. Marathon running in his early 20s has wrecked his knee. Phil's goal is to find something that will replace running to keep him fit, as his longer-term health depends on it. This is a deficit goal to improve his current poorer health.

Sometimes we set goals that come out of a personal or professional desire to improve some element of our life. It's not imposed on us: it's of our own free will and we feel we're in charge of our decision. Sometimes it feels as if goals are set for us. We're told we need to change our eating, drinking or lifestyle habits for our own good health. We're made redundant and encouraged to look for another job. We're set targets for our key performance indicators or personal development plans.

What is the impact of those different reasons for setting goals? Look back at your list of goals. How many are your own, how many do you feel you 'should' do?

Clear the SMOG

When setting goals and considering what we are going to think, feel and do to make them happen, it's helpful to recognize when we're working in a SMOG. Do any of these sound familiar?

- I *should* cut back on the red wine.
- I *must* talk to my boss about that report.
- I *ought* to exercise more.
- I've *got* to stop procrastinating.

SMOG (should, must, ought and got to) gets in the way of our ability to achieve our goals – after each of those statements, the obvious word is 'but'. We need to cut through the SMOG because if it lingers and the 'but' gets in the way, our chances of success are limited.

In all of these instances, the goals are not ours. Someone, be it friend, family member, colleague, boss or expert, has influenced our thinking about the goal. The goal is what we think we *should*, *must* or *ought* to be doing, not what we *want* to be doing. If we set a goal that has little or no excitement or drive for us, it's going to be a tough road to achieve it. Finding the reason, the emotional connection for setting the goal, is the key to unlocking our ability to achieve it, and to align our attitudes and behaviours with our personal values and guiding principles.

CONNECT EMOTIONALLY WITH YOUR GOALS

If we think of the EI scales discussed earlier in the book, we can now look at how they can link together. When you are high in those scales, the likelihood is that you'll get to where you want to be.

As in all things, the individual's level of self-regard is crucial. If you believe in yourself, and have a high sense of worth, you will believe that you deserve the very best that life can bring, and will draw success towards you. Combined with a strong regard for others, there's more chance you'll be able to achieve your goals and have a positive impact on others along the way. Knowing our values, our guiding principles, and using our emotional intelligence when we're setting our goals, creates a much higher chance that we'll get to where we want to be.

Some of the individual effectiveness scales are directly linked with setting and achieving goals. Someone with a high sense of personal power (how much you take control of your life, seeing yourself as responsible for your own actions) will be able to take responsibility for what he or she does. This applies to both the things that work well *and* those that don't go the way he or she wants them to. How often do people blame others when things don't work out? How often is it 'someone else's fault'?

Whose targets?

Debbie is a sales assistant for a mobile phone company. She is set rigorous targets each month and her income is both salary and commission based.

Each month Debbie misses her targets by a small percentage, reducing the amount of commission she receives, and every month when her boss, Daniel, gets her into his office to ask her what she could do differently to hit that target, she makes the same comment: 'Don't blame me, I'm doing my best – I didn't set the targets.'

What impact can this attitude have on Debbie's behaviour? Let's imagine what she might feel, think and do; see Figure 8.1.

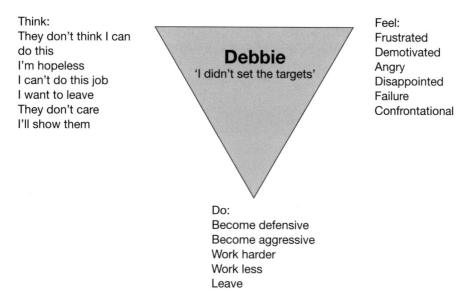

Think:
They don't think I can do this
I'm hopeless
I can't do this job
I want to leave
They don't care
I'll show them

Debbie
'I didn't set the targets'

Feel:
Frustrated
Demotivated
Angry
Disappointed
Failure
Confrontational

Do:
Become defensive
Become aggressive
Work harder
Work less
Leave

Figure 8.1   Debbie and her targets

Sometimes we are in charge of our own goals and our own targets, but there are also many times when we work to company goals and organizational and team targets. If we believe we have no personal power over those 'external' goals, we may find it harder to work towards them, and our behaviour will reflect the lack of power and control that we may feel.

So what's the answer? Let's look at Debbie's situation again, and see how her line manager could ask coaching questions to help her:

Debbie: Don't blame me, I'm doing my best – *I* didn't set the targets!
Dan: I know you've worked hard this month Debbie. What's helped you get to the figures you've achieved?
Debbie: Well, I guess I was just lucky with some of the customers who came in, but it's so frustrating. Every month it's just out of my reach; it's always the same.

Dan: What targets would you set yourself then, Debbie, if you could?

Debbie: That's daft, because I can't set my own targets, that's not how it works here!

Dan: But if you could?

Debbie: Well, I suppose I'd set them just a little bit lower, then they'd be achievable.

Dan: What else could you do?

Debbie: Well, I suppose I could tell myself I'll go the extra mile one month and see if I can achieve them.

Dan: What would it be like to reach those targets next month?

Debbie: It'd be fantastic! I'd feel like I'd actually achieved something. It'd be great to be able to show them I can do it!

Dan: What would be fantastic about it? What would you get from achieving them?

Debbie: I'd feel successful, I'd know I'd done a good job, and I'd feel I'd contributed to the store's success.

Dan: So what might you do differently next month, to help you achieve your target and contribute to all our success?

Debbie: Could we do something in store for our customers? Something to get more people in here? I'm sure I could lift my sales if that happened.

Dan: How about you put some ideas together and we can all talk them through?

What's the impact on Debbie's sense of personal power? How has Dan helped her see there's a different way of approaching her targets? We'll look in more detail at how values impact on the goal-setting process, and how if we play to our strengths we can influence the levels of success we achieve.

If our goal-directedness scale (how clear we are on our goals, and how much our attitudes, beliefs and actions support us by moving us towards these goals) is high, we're going to be more able to set goals that are aligned to our values because we understand how important that is to us, and we know how to get there. Our behaviour will support the goal and we're more likely to do something every day to move us towards it. In Debbie's case, high goal directedness would undoubtedly have helped her focus on reaching her targets and finding ways of doing it, because they would have been in her plans each day.

Flexibility (how free you feel to adapt your thoughts, attitudes and behaviour in times of change) can work with or against successful goal setting. Being high in flexibility can mean that we could swing with the wind and lose focus. If our self-awareness is good and if we are aware of the impact of the loss of focus, and that we can play to our strengths, then flexibility can help us see different ways to get to our goals. We are prepared to try something different and get to the destination via a different route. Debbie may have come up with some ideas about customer engagement, she may have realized earlier in the month that her figures were low, and changed her sales strategy earlier.

Our levels on the self-management scale of emotional resilience (how well you bounce back when things go wrong) contribute to the way we get over the perceived lack of success in reaching our goals. How do you bounce back when things don't go your way? Working with her emotional resilience and personal power, Debbie could have seen how she could use her strengths to do something differently.

If you set off on holiday in a motorhome, looking forward to the freedom and spontaneity that being in charge of your own accommodation and location brings, and then the camper van breaks down, how would you deal with it? The emotionally unintelligent holidaymakers may throw the towel in, get the breakdown van to take the motorhome back home and spend the rest of the holiday back at home fuming and sulking, complaining about the unreliability of the motorhome and missing out on the holiday. The emotionally intelligent holidaymakers, however, may engage their personal power and realize that they still have a say in what happens next. Their flexibility would let them see that there could be something to be gained from the situation anyway. They could have the motorhome towed to the campsite (saving fuel) and then get it repaired on site, or even replace it with a newer model for the journey home. Their resilience would help them see the positive side and think of an ingenious solution to the 'problem'.

IT'S ALL ABOUT MIND OVER MATTER

What attitudes do you have that help you achieve your goals? What do you believe about your ability to stick at something until you get there? What helps or hinders you as you set yourself goals and move towards your dreams?

Self-efficacy means the degree to which we believe in ourselves and our capabilities, whether it's in our ability to achieve goals or be a great coach. It's self-esteem and self-confidence rolled into one: how much we believe in who we are and what we do.

When we're setting goals, we're advised to make them achievable, but what does that mean? How does that differ from their being realistic? Whose definition of achievable are we working with? If we have an attitude that, 'I never achieve my goals' it doesn't matter how 'achievable' we make them: our attitude may kick in unconsciously and sabotage any chance we have of hitting the target!

Be careful what you believe, think about or say to yourself!

Bob's plough

Bill, a farmer, needed to plough his field before the dry spell set in, but his own plough had broken.

'I know, I'll ask my neighbour, farmer Bob, to borrow his plough. He's a good man; I'm sure he'll have done his ploughing by now and he'll be happy to lend me his machine.'

So Bill began to walk the three or four fields to Bob's farm. After a field of walking, Bill says to himself, 'I hope that Bob has finished all his own ploughing or he'll not be able to lend me his machine.'

Then after a few more minutes of worrying and walking, Bill says to himself, 'And what if Bob's plough is old and on its last legs – he'll never want to lend it to me, will he?'

After another field, Bill says, 'Bob was never a very helpful fellow, I reckon maybe he won't be too keen to lend me his plough even if it's in perfect working order and he's finished all his own ploughing weeks ago.'

As Bill arrives at Bob's farm, Bill is thinking, 'That old Bob can be a mean old fellow. I reckon even if he's got all his ploughing done, and his own machine is sitting there doing nothing, he'll not lend it to me just to watch me go to ruin.'

Bill walks up Bob's front path, knocks on the door, and Bob answers. 'Well good morning Bill, what can I do for you?' asks Bob with a smile.

And Bill says, with eyes bulging, 'You can take your wretched plough, and you can stick it where the sun doesn't shine!'

> *To accomplish great things, we must not only act, but also dream; not only plan, but also believe.*
>
> Anatole France

We need to engage our positive attitudes or change our negative ones in order to give goal achievement any chance at all. We must also work out whether the goals we set ourselves are in line with our values, or better still, check our values before we set our goals.

Think of a salesperson who lists 'love' at the top of their values and 'well-being' second. They have a goal of being the top salesperson in their field, earning £200,000 per annum because they want the best for their family. They want to be able to give them opportunities and experiences and spend plenty of quality time as a family. To achieve the goal, they choose to travel for 10 months of the year, working 14-hour days, eating fast food for lunch and having business dinners with clients in the evening. When they are at home, they play golf with the MD and the rest of the time they sleep or watch TV. They feel exhausted at the end of each week, they hardly see their family and the weekends fly by.

What conflict exists here? Sometimes we're distracted by things that seem to be on our goal list, maybe a healthy salary and bank balance in this case. Having the awareness to recognize whether our goals support our values will help remove the distraction, making it easier to make decisions that work for us.

IS WORKING SMARTER THE ONLY WAY?

The EI coach will be instrumental in helping coachees set dynamic, congruent goals. Ethical EI coaches know that they'll also use their skills as well as their attitudes and habits in their own business and personal lives by setting goals that are in alignment with their own values.

Goal-setting formulae and acronyms have been in the business world for many years, but what about setting and achieving goals the emotionally intelligent way? When working with coachees, having techniques such as effective goal-setting tools at your fingertips can both simplify the process and raise the level of performance.

SMART goal setting is well known, and there are variations on a theme, but the main principle is to make any goal:

Specific,
Measurable,
Attractive or Achievable,
Realistic, and
Time framed.

This goal-setting process has its place; it can keep goal-setting time to a minimum by ensuring every box is ticked, which predominantly works best in a business setting. However, it lacks one crucial 'check box', that of values, whether personal or business values. There is also the possibility of creating and working towards a personal goal with negative language such as giving up smoking, losing weight, etc.

VALID goal setting

We have developed an EI goal-setting model that takes into account our values, attitudes and habits, working with our strengths to raise the likelihood of our achieving what we set out to achieve. The benefit of this model is that it engages our emotional brain as well as our thinking brain, and we know from research that everything we do is influenced heavily by our emotional brain.

If we break down the elements of the VALID model, we can see how it can support any other formula and framework within the personal or organizational goal-setting process:

- *V*alues: understand what is really important about this goal, what will be great about achieving it in the grand scheme of things.
- *A*ttitudes: check that your positive attitudes and beliefs will support and be supported by your values. What you do will also impact on your attitude. High self-regard and regard for others underpins positive attitudes.
- *A*wareness: helps coachees raise their self-awareness as to what they think, feel and do towards reaching their goal. This will increase their ability to monitor their progress, note when things get in the way, and help them make decisions about what to do to get back on track. Including awareness in the goal-setting process in an organizational setting can be in the form of regular update reports or meetings, checking against progress.
- *L*ikely: asking, 'How likely is it that you will achieve the goal?' is again a great awareness-raising question. Is it achievable? Is it realistic? How does it link in with your outlook on life? Are you optimistic, pessimistic, or is your outlook balanced and realistic?
- *I*ntention: our intention is linked strongly to our values. If we know why we're working towards this goal, we can use our strengths, personal power and flexibility to keep on track.
- *D*o: consider what behaviour will help you achieve it. Is there anything you want to do differently from your default setting that will really make reaching this goal more successful? Positive behaviours will strengthen your positive attitudes and fulfil your personal values.
- *D*one date: give your goal a deadline! It improves the chances of success to know when you'll be in the new situation.

Activity: VALID

Take one of the goals you noted down earlier in the Be, Do, Have activity and consider the following questions in the VALID model:

My goal is: _____

- V. What's really important to you about achieving this goal? What values do you hold that this goal will support and fulfil? When you reach it, what do you expect to feel? What do you expect to think? How will life feel great?
- A. What attitudes and beliefs do you have that will help you succeed in achieving this goal? What attitudes and beliefs do you have that may hinder you as you move forward? What do you want to do about that?
- A. What do you feel when you think about working towards this goal? Where do you feel it? What is your intuition telling you?
- L. Is your goal achievable? Is it realistic? What might get in the way? What will make it happen?
- I. How strong is your intention to achieve this? What strengths do you possess that will help you? Where do you have influence and personal power?
- D. What will you do to achieve your goal? What is your action plan? What is your first step?
- D. What is your timeline for this goal? Is it a long-, short- or medium-term goal? How will you celebrate achieving your goal on that date?

What helps goals become reality? Is it purely luck? Is it sheer grit and perseverance? How come some people can be apparently more successful at achieving their goals than others?

The Institute for Applied Emotional Intelligence did research into the chances of our completing our goals. Their findings (Wiseman, 2004) were these:

- You have an idea – 10 per cent.
- Decide when you will do it – 40 per cent.
- Plan how you will do it – 50 per cent.
- Commit to someone else you will do it – 65 per cent.
- Have a specific accountability appointment with the person you've committed to – 95 per cent.

We know from research that our limbic brain has around 6 billion nerve cells firing each second, and that our logical brain has about 100 neuronal stimulations. Every second, messages are being fired from our brain all around our body. Imagine that you're in a busy railway station. There's a lot of noise around you – passenger announcements, people talking, music, traffic noise maybe. How much do you really notice? Not much; it probably feels like a general background noise. But then a new passenger announcement is made, telling you of a delay to your train's departure. Suddenly your attention is switched on. Your reticular activating system

(RAS) has kicked in. This is the automatic filter inside your brain that brings relevant information to your attention. It's like a filter passing information from the conscious mind to your unconscious mind.

Have you ever decided to buy something, thinking it was unusual? Maybe a car in a colour you don't see often and then once you've bought it, you see lots of them about? Of course all of those cars were around before, you just never noticed because it wasn't on your radar.

Spotting gorillas

Harvard psychologist Daniel Simons made a 30-second film in the late 1990s to study the psychology of vision, which demonstrates the power of our mind to focus in on something so powerfully that we completely ignore and miss other things around it. The film shows six basketball players; three in white T-shirts, three in black T-shirts. The white T-shirted players pass the basketball between one another. Halfway through the film, a man in a gorilla suit wanders on, saunters through the players, does a gorilla chest pound at the camera and then walks off the court.

The volunteers in the study are asked to count the number of times the white T-shirted players pass the ball, and at the end of the film are then asked if they noticed anything unusual. Very few people see anything out of the ordinary! When they were shown the film a second time, they were amazed to see the gorilla that they had completely missed before.

If you use your RAS's power with goal setting, you have a heady mix. You will start to look for evidence that supports your actions towards your goals. You will start to notice things around you you'd never noticed before.

When we're working with coachees to help them move forward, achieve their goals and feel fulfilled, there are several techniques that can help them match their goals with their values.

Activity: Your ideal day

Imagine you have a day away from your usual routine. No work to do, no commitments, no time pressures. You have unlimited resources and the power to do absolutely anything you would like to for a full day.

What do you do? Take some time to consider what you would do if you could create your ideal day. Who would be with you, where would you be, what would you do?

What do you feel during this day? Write down your emotions and sensations; make it feel real. What's in your mind, what are you thinking?

GOALS ARE VEHICLES FOR LIVING OUR VALUES

If you're a coach you'll be well aware of your values. If you've worked through the exercises in Chapter 6, you'll have a good idea of what guides you, what motivates you and what's going on when your life feels great.

Activity

Write your values down here:

1.
2.
3.
4.
5.
6.

Referring back to the 'Your ideal day' activity, which of those activities reflect these values? When you're experiencing positive emotions, do they connect with any of your values?

When we're working with coachees, helping them to check each goal they set against their values will raise the bar on the chances of success. The EI coach will check in with the attitudes their coachees hold that may help or hinder their progress towards their goals, working with their strengths to support areas that might get in the way of success.

HOW GOALS FLOW FROM VALUES TO ACTION

Within organizations and in our own lives we may find ourselves working to someone else's agenda. This can have many different effects, not least the sense of frustration and sometimes anger that it's not our aim, not our wish.

We always have a choice!

We can let this choice affect our behaviour and our performance. Remember the equation $P = p - i$? Performance equals potential minus interference. Our blind resistance to a goal that others have set becomes a huge interference and impacts massively on our performance ability. We can also let it affect our behaviour in a positive way by finding what matters to us about the goal. If it's one that's 'imposed' upon us, there may still be something in there that can be linked to our own personal motivators. We may have to dig for it, but the rewards are worth it.

Let's consider Debbie the sales assistant who misses her targets and feels powerless to make any choice about her targets. Debbie's targets are set for her, and she feels unable to do anything about them. She blames others when she doesn't achieve them, saying they are too high, too unrealistic and it's simply not fair. What could Debbie do to take back some ownership of those targets? How could she link them with something that really matters to her, and what impact might that have?

In the coaching scenario we considered earlier in the chapter, there was a shift for Debbie when she thought about what she would do if she were in charge of the targets. She began to take back some of her personal power, and it energized her thinking. When we feel powerless, it seems that our emotional brain disconnects from seeking a solution. Retrieving an element of influence over the situation kick-starts our solution-seeking.

Debbie starts to bounce back from feeling frustrated and even angry. She begins to think in a different way, coming to the problem from a different angle. She begins to find solutions. Her attitudes are being challenged, especially the attitude about her personal power (the degree to which she believes she is in charge of what happens in her life), and she has sole responsibility for her behaviour.

Her line manager asks her questions about what's important. For example, what would be fantastic about achieving her targets the next month, and elicits the response that she'd feel successful, that she'd done a good job and made a contribution. Once she begins to engage with the new perspective, she can start to shift her thinking and begin to find solutions that work for her. The organization's goal hasn't changed. Debbie will still have similar performance targets, but now she's developing an attitude of personal power, and linking in with what's important to her. Her behaviour will begin to support these attitudes and beliefs, and her performance will almost certainly improve. She's beginning to remove the interferences.

If we look at the process in more detail, we can see how the EI coach can begin to formulate questions and a framework for working with coachees to help them set authentic goals that support their values. The coachees can set exciting goals that are underpinned by emotionally intelligent attitudes and explore behaviours that help them move towards their goals every single day.

The Goal Flow Map

The Goal Flow Map is a diagram or illustration of the process showing the impact of setting goals that are either in line with our values and attitudes or out of line with them; see Figure 8.2. The connection between values, attitudes and behaviour is crucial to the success of any goal. The cumulative effect of constantly setting goals that are supported by our values is that we will build strong neuronal pathways of positive attitudes. This will lead to emotionally intelligent behaviours that will bring happiness, success and good health.

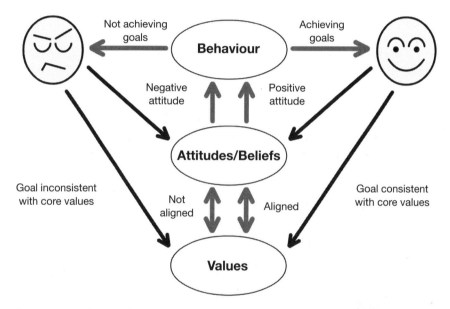

Figure 8.2   The Goal Flow Map

The cumulative effect of constantly setting goals that are *not* supported by our values is lack of fulfilment and satisfaction. The negative attitudes we may hold are reinforced, our negative attitudes impact on our behaviour and the chances of achieving our goals drop. That lack of success then compounds the negative attitude, and the spiral starts again. We'll feel frustrated because the goals are in conflict with our values.

How would Debbie's conversation go if it had been with an EI coach? How would knowledge of the Goal Flow Map impact on the conversation?

Debbie: Don't blame me, I'm doing my best – *I* didn't set the targets!
Coach: I know you've worked hard this month Debbie. What's helped you get to the figures you've achieved?

Debbie: Well, I guess I was just lucky with some of the customers who came in, but it's so frustrating. Every month it's just out of my reach, it's always the same.

Coach: What targets would you set yourself then, Debbie, if you could?

Debbie: That's daft, because I can't set my own targets. That's not how it works here!

Coach: But if you could?

Debbie: Well, I suppose I'd set them just a little bit lower, then they'd be achievable.

Coach: What would it be like to reach those targets next month?

Debbie: It'd be fantastic! I'd feel like I'd actually achieved something, it'd be great to be able to show them I can do it!

Coach: What would be fantastic about it? What would you get from achieving them?

Debbie: I'd feel successful, I'd know I'd done a good job, and I'd feel I'd contributed to the store's success.

Coach: What would success feel like Debbie?

Debbie: It would feel invigorating; I'd be full of energy.

Coach: What's important about being able to show others you can do it?

Debbie: I think it's important to be recognized for putting time and effort into something. I'd not realized that one of the reasons I'm so frustrated about missing my targets is that nobody comments on the things I do well, and I like to be appreciated! Doesn't everybody?

Coach: Tell me about contribution. You commented you'd feel you'd contributed to the store's success....

Debbie: Well, we're a team, and it's good when the team achieves, and I like to be part of that. I guess if I remember that reaching my targets also benefits the whole store, it might inspire me to put in that one extra degree!

Debbie has started to link the targets with her own personal values. She's beginning to see how putting in the effort to reach those goals would actually support what's important to her. It would help her live her values. How might it go from here?

Coach: From what you've told me here Debbie, what would you say motivates you to achieve those targets?

Debbie: I think contributing to the team success, being recognized for having achieved my own personal targets and the sense of a job well done would be the motivators.

Coach: Right at the beginning of our conversation you expressed frustration that your targets are always out of reach, and that you have no say in them. What do you have a say in?

Debbie: Well, I suppose I'm realizing I could put in more effort, and also I could come up with some creative ideas. I like being creative!
Coach: What else do you have a say in?
Debbie: I guess, how wound up I get. It doesn't really help anyone!
Coach: What else do you notice about yourself when you feel frustrated?
Debbie: I stop thinking clearly, I don't put in as much effort, I probably don't even talk to the customers as pleasantly!

The coach has now enabled Debbie to understand more about how she responds and what she feels in the situation. She's now beginning to see that she does have a considerable amount of 'control' over the situation.

The coach now begins to get underneath Debbie's attitudes:

Coach: What's going to make the difference here?
Debbie: I'm not sure whether I can actually up my game enough.
Coach: What's prompting you to think that?
Debbie: Well, I've not yet achieved my targets this year. I'm not sure whether I can!
Coach: When have you achieved your goals?
Debbie: Well, it's not related, but I did manage to win the tennis tournament last year! But that's different.
Coach: How is it different?
Debbie: (after some consideration) Maybe it's not that different. I thought I wouldn't be able to do it, but I really wanted to win, so talked myself into it pretty much.
Coach: What else?
Debbie: I put in a lot of practice and spent some time with the tennis coach, learning from him.
Coach: So what might you take from that experience?
Debbie: I could review how I sell at the moment, and perhaps ask my colleagues for some pointers. They'd quite like that, actually!

Debbie's now getting underneath some of the beliefs that have possibly held her back unconsciously. Now she's looking for different ways to do things, she's seeing all sorts of opportunities. She's beginning to spot some gorillas!

The final piece in the goal flow jigsaw is the behaviours. What does Debbie need to do to achieve her targets? What positive behaviours might she want to develop in order to get there?

Coach: Let's look at what you do, Debbie, when you're up against it. What do you do when you're frustrated with your perceived lack of success?

Debbie: I get quite aggressive I think, not physically, but I start to shout or
          might even be a bit rude! I think my frustration probably shows
          because I don't smile as much, and people do comment on that. I
          usually snap at them then. I think I might also stop trying. I usually
          end up thinking, 'Here we go again, another month below target'
          and give up.
Coach: What could be different?
Debbie: I could remember this conversation! Being stroppy and giving up
          really doesn't help me at all.
Coach: So what are you going to do?
Debbie: I'm going to notice when I start to panic about my sales figures
          and I'm going to remind myself that I'm more successful when I'm
          relaxed. I'm going to see how I can be creative in ways to get more
          customers to buy.

Debbie is now aligning her goals with her values. She understands more
about how she responds when she's up against it by raising her awareness
about how she responds both emotionally and physically in that situation.
She is beginning to engage her emotional intelligence to help her achieve the
targets set for her by setting goals for herself. She's regaining her personal
power.

By setting goals in this way, and noticing what works well in achieving
them, coachees will develop strong positive attitudes, replacing old, unhelp-
ful negative ones. This will impact positively on their self-regard and self-
belief, further building their emotional intelligence and understanding of
themselves.

It builds on the principle behind EI, which is the habitual practice of using
emotional information from ourselves and other people and integrating this
with our thinking. We then use this to inform our decision making to help us
get what we want from the immediate situation and from life in general.

In order to act with emotional intelligence, writes Tim Sparrow (Sparrow
and Knight, 2006), we need to notice our feelings, pay attention to them and
give them significance. We need to think about them and take them into
account in choosing what to do. This applies both to our own feelings and
those of others.

We would also include checking our values. How do our actions and
thoughts support our values? Where might there be conflict? When we notice
our thinking and feeling, and link them with our values before we act, we
give ourselves the best chance of living congruent lives around congruent
goals.

What's the impact of constantly not achieving your goals, or of working
towards goals that are not congruent with your values? This can impact on
health. As we saw in the values chapter, if we live in conflict with our values

it can have a physical impact on us, causing stress and real dissatisfaction, leading to emotional strain. It can also knock confidence. You can begin to feel things always go wrong for you and that whatever you try is destined to fail.

It will start to build and reinforce negative attitudes around 'I can't achieve my goals' and may impact on your goal directedness and sense of personal responsibility. Also, you'll be reluctant to set goals. How many people do you know who have said, 'I don't set New Year's resolutions any more, there's no point, they don't work'? It's not the resolutions that don't work; it's the fact that we set the wrong resolutions or have the wrong attitude and values underpinning the resolution.

We can link attitudes, values, goals and behaviour to the thinking, feeling, doing triangle, shown in Figure 8.3. EI coaches can then ask questions about the different elements of the triangle to support their coachees in their goal setting and achievement.

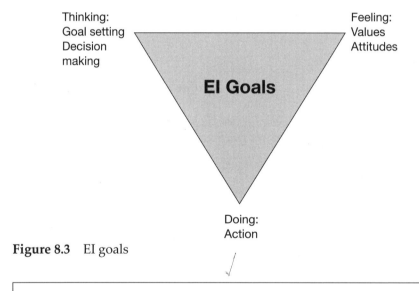

Figure 8.3   EI goals

Summary

- Set goals, vision or plans for the future in line with your values and guiding principles. If they aren't, you run the risk of working towards a future that isn't really going to work for you.
- Everything starts from an emotion. Check your goals against your feeling and thinking.
- Connect emotionally with your goals.
- Notice and practise behaviour and habits that will help you achieve your goals.

- Build strong positive attitudes and beliefs that will support your values and lead to your achieving your goals.
- It really is all about mind over matter!
- Raise your self-awareness so you notice when your goals are in line with your values.
- Values, attitudes and behaviour support and build each other whether negatively or positively, depending on their alignment.
- When working with coachees, look for the values underneath the goal.
- Ask thinking, feeling, doing questions in the goal-setting process.
- Use the Goal Flow Map as a structure within a coaching session.
- The VALID goal-setting process – structuring goal setting around values, attitudes, likelihood of success, intention and focus and a deadline – contributes to goal setting that engages the emotional brain and gives a higher chance of success.
- Goals are vehicles for living our values.

References

Simons, D J and Chabris, C F (1999) Gorillas in our midst: sustained inattentional blindness for dynamic events, *Perception*, **28**, pp 1059–74

Sparrow, T and Knight, A (2006) *Applied EI*, Wiley, Chichester

Wiseman, R (2004) *Did You Spot the Gorilla?*, Arrow Books, London

9

The coaching toolkit

> *As a psychologist when EI was popularized I thought 'finally you can talk about feelings; now's there's a science to it and research behind it — it's key. I was thrilled that it came in the market place — a way to improve and measure how I am. The old attitude of 'leave your emotions at home' — that control and command style is out of date. We are working with whole people and have to take emotions into account. EI is the missing link — it's what makes it sustainable.*
>
> Dr Patrick Williams, former Board Director of ICF and Board Director of Association of Coach Training Organizations in the United States

Even though you can develop your EI alone (and we looked at a number of tools to help you do this in Chapter 5), EI development is most effective when facilitated by a skilled, emotionally intelligent coach (an EI coach). As EI development is a very individual, personal journey that only the person developing him or herself knows exactly how to travel on, the non-directive nature of coaching provides an ideal partner to this change process.

The starting point to this relationship is to find out where the coachees are right now, and the easiest way to do that is to get them to measure their EI and use the results for the starting point for change. However, measuring EI using the individual effectiveness^{TM} tool is unlike many other measures available. Many psychometric tools, such as the MBTI, require the facilitator to be an expert, giving feedback to coachees on what their strengths are and what they need to change. With effective EI measurement, coachees look at the results and select the areas for change themselves (see Figure 9.1). This 'I'm ok, you're ok', adult-adult approach is, in our opinion, more effective than much of the parent-child measurement that takes place with some psychometric measures. (The coach/psychologist is the expert telling the coachee what they need to develop.)

4. Chosen change achieved, development of new habits
(in coachee)

3. Implementation of change plan (by coachee)

2. Selection of areas to change (by coachee)

1. Increase self-knowledge in (coachee)

Figure 9.1   The EI model of change (adapted from Sparrow and Knight, 2006)

AGREEMENT AND CONTRACT

Once you have a measure of EI, it should provide some clear indicators for areas of development and targets during the coaching relationship. However, before the coaching starts, a clear contract needs to be set between the coach and coachee. Take a moment to think about this question: what needs to be agreed and discussed before coaching starts?

Here are some of the things we feel are important to consider in a coaching contracting session. (When we refer to 'contracting' here, this includes the verbal discussions the coach and coachee should have as well as any written, formal contract):

- What are the reasons for the coaching?
- What are the coachees' attitudes towards coaching?
- How does the coachee feel about coaching?
- Has the coachee done any coaching before? If so, what was the experience like for him or her?
- Have the coach and coachee established a good rapport? For example, if the coach is the coachee's manager, what is their working relationship like? Is this a suitable match?
- How committed is the coachee to coaching?
- What are the reporting and confidentiality boundaries and are these clearly understood by the coach and the coachee?
- How often will the coaching be and how long will each session be?
- Has the coachee allocated the time for coaching, both the actual sessions and the actions that come from the sessions?
- What is the contracted time for the coaching?
- What are the overall goals for the coaching? Are there specific performance-related goals and what are they?
- How will the impact of the coaching be measured? How will the coachee know that the coaching has been successful in achieving the goals set?
- How and when will the coaching be reviewed?

Here is a model coaching contract to give you an example of the type of agreement you could use.

Coaching Agreement

Between _____ (Coachee)

and _____ (Coach)

In undertaking to coach you I am committing myself to being available at the time(s) we agree on and to providing a trusting, confidential relationship for you to explore issues and difficulties and move towards change. I will endeavour to support you in this process.

In undertaking to receive coaching from me you are committing yourself to being open and honest and agreeing to be committed to optimizing the use of the coaching time. Your intent to grow in excellence and develop is a key ingredient in a successful coaching experience.

To be coachable, you must ensure that:

- Your intent to change and desire for change are serious.
- You are willing to try new ways of learning, be truthful, keep to your commitments and inform your coach immediately when things are not working for you.
- You are willing to explore, challenge and change thoughts, feelings and actions if you feel it will be beneficial for you.
- You understand that your coach will be focused on you, your goals and your best interests. Your coach will be non-directive and non-judgemental.

Confidentiality

The coaching service is confidential between the coach and the coachee except in the following instances:

- It has been agreed in advance that the progress of the sessions will be discussed with senior management.
- If the coachee gives the coach information for the purpose of discussion with others.
- If the coachee gives the coach information which may be linked with possible physical harm to the coachee or others.

Cancellations

If you wish to change the time of a session the coach should be informed in writing as soon as possible and a minimum of three working days before the scheduled session. The full coaching fee will be charged for changes made less than three days in advance.

Duration and termination

The initial coaching agreement is for: _____

Towards the end of these sessions there will be a discussion regarding progression and next steps. Termination of coaching should be in writing and agreed before the final coaching session to allow time for closure.

Coachee records

Any written notes taken by the coach are securely kept and are confidential.

I have read and understood this agreement.

Name: _____ (Coachee)

Signature: _____

Date: _____

Name: _____ (Coach)

Signature: _____

Date: _____

Code of ethics

We look at the purpose of a code of ethics in the next chapter – here is a sample EI code of ethics.

Code of ethics

I abide by this Code of Ethics and seek to:

- constantly improve my own performance and results;
- adhere to proper conduct regarding confidentiality;
- act in an accountable way with my colleagues, clients and coachees;
- make clear, concise contracts with my colleagues, clients and coachees;
- commit to ongoing learning and development;
- continually develop my own skills, knowledge, habits and attitudes in emotional intelligence and related fields.

Regarding my performance in the measurement and/or application of emotional intelligence I will commit to having a high level of:

- self-knowledge;
- emotional competencies;
- personal adaptability;
- knowledge concerning emotional conditions and dynamics in individuals and teams.

I will operate in ways that create mutual benefit by being:

- collaborative;
- creative;
- open to diversity and difference;
- accepting;
- respectfully challenging;
- open to feedback.

I will structure and manage development programmes in ways that:

> - create trust;
> - promote mutual benefit and respect;
> - demonstrate acceptance and support for both the individuals and the organizations I work for.

I will practise reflective learning and will undertake this in my professional work through processes such as:

> - review interviews;
> - peer supervision;
> - mentoring arrangements with experienced senior practitioners.

Here is a quick checklist of things to discuss at the first coach-coachee meeting, before any coaching starts.

First meeting checklist

Think, feel and do

- What thoughts has the coachee got about the coaching?
- How does he or she feel about the coaching (nervous, excited, apprehensive, bored, curious, relaxed, etc)?
- What is the coaching going to do for the coachee? What are the aims of the coaching sessions?

Reporting procedures, confidentiality and trust

- How well does the coachee trust the coach?
- What feelings and attitudes does he or she have connected to trust?
- Who will the coach or coachee be reporting to about the coaching (eg, senior manager)?
- Exactly what will be reported and what won't be reported?
- What does confidentiality mean in this relationship?
- Where will records be kept and who will have access to them?

Explanation of coaching style
- What does the coachee think coaching is?
- What are his or her expectations of what the coach will do and how he or she will do it?

Commitment
- What feelings has the coachee got towards changing attitudes, thoughts and actions?
- On a scale of 1 to 10, how committed is the coachee to change?
- What could be a barrier to commitment and change and how will the coachee overcome this?

Meeting arrangements and environment
- How often will the coaching take place?
- Where will the coaching take place?
- Can the coachee make sure he or she can secure a quiet, confidential, undisturbed space for each coaching session?
- Will the coaching be face-to-face, by phone, by e-mail or a combination?

The agreement/contract
- Have both the coach and coachee read and understood the contract?
- How did the coachee feel when he or she read the contract and signed it?

Finding focus

When agreeing on goals for the coaching, using a chart like the one in Table 9.1 should help the coachee to focus on his or her initial aims. Complete the finding focus table, being as specific as possible (we have completed the first boxes with an example).

Coaching preparation form

It's a great idea for coaches to encourage their coachees to prepare for each session, and the following form will help them consider their thoughts, feelings and actions in relation to the coaching.

Table 9.1   Finding focus table

Main area to focus on	What are my current thoughts about this?	What are my current feelings about this?	What are my current actions related to this?	Visualization of success (what am I thinking, feeling and doing?)
Become a better presenter	I don't like presenting. I am not made to be a presenter. I look too fat and people will notice this.	Nervous Anxious Irritated Sad Excited	My voice quivers. Sometimes my left leg starts to shake. I often forget my content. I am fixed to the spot.	I am standing upright, with a clear confident voice. My content is clear and I move around confidently. I feel great, full of energy and am motivating the audience who are all smiling and listening intently.

Preparation form

So that we can maximize the time we spend together, please take the time to complete this form before the coaching session.

What worked well for me during our last session? How did I feel during the session? What did I think? What did I do in connection with the session?

What have I accomplished since our last session? How do I feel about this? What thoughts were connected to this?

What didn't I get done, but intended to? How do I feel about this? What thoughts were connected to this?

What challenges am I facing now?

What opportunities are available to me right now?

What are my thoughts about my next coaching session?

What am I feeling about this session?

What do I want to use my coach for during the session?

Think, feel and do wheels

Using a wheel is a good way of getting an overview of the areas a coachee wants to change. The starting point is to think of specific areas of behaviour to change and then to ask the coachee open questions to elicit the current thoughts and feeling the coachee has connected to that action. An example, with the first part already filled in, is shown in Figure 9.2.

Figure 9.2 Think, feel and do wheel

COACHING MODELS

The EI COACH model

(A detailed explanation of this model and how to use it is given in Chapter 7); the acronym stands for:

E = Emotions (how are you feeling?)
I = Intelligence (What do you want to talk about and achieve today?)
C = Current
O = Opportunities
A = Actions
C = measure of Change
H = How are you feeling now?

The PAUSE model

The PAUSE model can be used to focus on one specific behaviour or habit change, helping coachees understand their feelings and thoughts in the moment when they perform the habit.

First identify the specific behaviour the coachee wants to change then go through the following stages of open questions:

P = *Pause.* Stop and think about the moment you are doing the behaviour right now.
A = *Attitude and emotion.* What are you feeling? Where are you feeling it in your body? What attitudes are connected to these feelings?
U = *Understand.* Why are these thoughts, feelings and actions not benefiting you? What will be the advantages of changing? What has stopped you changing until now and how will you make sure it doesn't stop you in the future?
S = *Specific behaviour change.* Visualize the specific behaviour change you will achieve. How do you feel? What are you thinking? How is your behaviour different? Repeat this specific visualization every day for the next 21 days.
E = *Evaluate.* How will you know when you have successfully replaced your old habit with a new, more effective habit?

Challenging and changing attitudes and behaviour

This activity works well for a coach working with his or her coachee towards an attitude change.

Choose one attitude you would like to change:

Can you think of a real-life situation that in some way is connected to this attitude? How did you behave in this situation? What did you think in this situation? What were you feeling at the time?

What are all the things you could do to change this? (No limits here – the solutions do not have to be realistic.)
What else could you do?
If you were giving someone else advice on what he or she could do differently in this situation, what would you tell him or her?
If you had a magic wand you could wave to make you think, feel and behave perfectly in the situation, describe how your thoughts, feelings and actions would be different.

Which of these solutions is the best and most realistic for you right now?

What are all the things that need to happen for you to achieve this?

What's the first step?

When are you going to do this?

How will you measure whether you have achieved this first step successfully?

Are you happy to let me know?
When and how will you do this?

Understanding goals

In Chapter 8 we introduced our Goal Flow Map; reproduced here in Figure 9.3. This formula can also be used as a very effective coaching tool, helping coachees to understand what is currently preventing them from achieving their goals, or understanding why they are not happy if they are achieving their goals. The connection between values and goals is best made after the coach has carried out a values elicitation with the coachee (see Chapter 6).

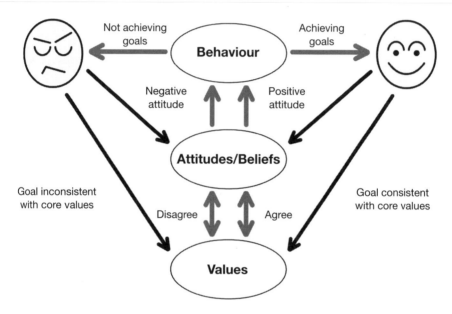

Figure 9.3   The Goal Flow Map

The coach asks a number of open questions connected to the coachee's behaviours, attitudes, beliefs and values connected to specific goals. This will help understanding of which level (or levels) of the formula is preventing the coachee reaching his or her goals. Here is an example:

Coachee goal: To stop smoking
Behaviour: What have you done so far to help you stop?
Attitudes: What are your attitudes towards smoking? What do you believe about your reasons for smoking? What does smoking give you? What does it not give you?
Values: Your top three values are freedom, independence and having fun. How are they connected to your habit of smoking? In what ways is smoking in line with these values? In what ways does smoking disagree with these values?

COACHING QUESTIONS

Question types

One of the key tools EI coaches have at their disposal is effective questions. Here we summarize the main useful question types, but before we give you examples, why not test yourself and see if you can come up with several example questions for each of the categories shown in Table 9.2?

Table 9.2   Question types

Question Type	Example
Powerful questions Questions that knock the coachee off balance, challenging them to think about something in a very different way.	How would you advise someone else to do that? What if money wasn't a barrier, what would you do? Imagine you wake up in the morning and the problem is solved – describe to me how things are?
Open Encourage other person to give a full answer. Can't be answered by 'yes/no' answers.	Often begin with: who, when, what, where, how and why. What seems to be the problem? How did you meet? Why do you like your job?
Follow on Encourage speaker to provide more information.	Tell me more? What happened then? How did he react?
Probing Challenge the speaker to develop discussion, often to look at alternative solutions.	How does this solve the problem? What evidence is there? Is there another way you could look at this?
Evaluating alternatives Used to help the speaker to make choices and to reach agreement.	Which of the 2 options is best for you? On the one hand, you could stay here. On the other hand, it may be time to move. What do you think?

Using pauses well is a very valuable questioning technique. If you want to encourage someone to keep talking, it is often enough to look attentive and interested and keep quiet. This is probably quite a difficult skill for many of us!

The question types shown in Table 9.3 should be avoided.

Table 9.3   Types of questions to avoid

Question Type	Example
Leading Suggest to the listener what answer you expect. Sometimes deliberately manipulative.	I expect you're happy with my decision? So, you are more than willing to complete this task I presume? So I guess you are happy to let me know in the next coaching session?
Multiple Confusing, as they ask more than one question at the same time.	How did you feel at the time and what were you thinking? What could you have done differently and how and when would you have done it?
When 'Why' questions need to be used with care, as sometimes they can sound very accusing. Often as children we ask lots of 'why' questions and sometimes our poor parents get a little impatient and irritated. As a result, many of us develop unconscious negative attitudes about why questions in our emotional brain.	Why haven't you done this? Why is this late? Why didn't you tell me?

Habit change: developing the habit of asking questions for others

In normal, everyday situations, who do you ask questions for? The answer in most cases will be for yourself. Most of us have developed the habit of using questions to gain information that we will find beneficial in some way. However, in coaching situations this is different. An effective EI coach should be asking questions that will benefit the coachee.

Just like most things, asking questions that are for the benefit of the other person can be developed as a habit. Try focusing on the questions you ask for the next 21 days, each day trying to increase the number of questions you ask for the benefit of others with no obvious benefit to yourself. For example, 'What will I get?' is clearly a self-focused question, whereas 'How did you feel when he said that?' places more emphasis on the other person.

It is also a good habit to develop for coaches to regularly reflect on the questions they have asked in coaching sessions (recording sessions with your coachee's permission enables you to review all the questions you asked). The following reflective questions should help this:

- What powerful questions did I ask today?
- How many open questions did I ask compared to closed questions?
- Which questions would I change so they offered more benefit to the coachee?
- Which leading questions did I ask? What judgements was I making that led to me asking these questions?

Reference

Sparrow, T and Knight, A (2006) *Applied EI*, Wiley, Chichester

10

Coaching ethics and best practice

> *Coaching ethics: integrity in the moment of choice.*
>
> Allard de Jong

So far we've looked at how developing our emotional intelligence improves our performance and we've explored how the KASH model is crucial to behavioural change. We've already discussed how EI is the habitual practice of:

- using emotional information from ourselves and other people;
- integrating this with our thinking;
- using these to inform our decision making to help us get what we want from the immediate situation and from life in general.

EI has a powerful impact on our relationships, both those we have with ourselves and those that we have with those around us. It therefore makes absolute sense that EI has to be embedded in the way we work as coaches, the way we run our businesses and the way we contribute to the growth of the 'profession' as a whole.

Ethical coaching can be defined as demonstrating integrity in the moment of choice. It is engaging our awareness and emotional intelligence to ask the best question at any particular moment. It is using our high levels of regard for ourselves and others to keep judgement out of the equation and holding our belief in our abilities to coach, and our coachees' own abilities to get to where they want to be.

Working to a code of conduct that reflects how we coach, how we manage ourselves in the coaching relationship and how we manage the relationship between ourselves and our coachees is about living the life and profession of an EI coach. A coach working without observing best practice, without working to an ethical code and without engaging in his or her own personal and professional development is a bit like a tightrope walker. We may think we've got sufficient training and know what we're doing in all circumstances, but it only takes one slip, one unexpected hazard to surprise us, and we can be in all sorts of trouble!

As coaches we encourage our clients to become more aware of how they think, feel and behave if they are working within EI principles, and to take personal responsibility for themselves and their behaviour and attitudes. For the coach, it is also vitally important that we develop our own awareness and responsibility for our coaching practice and professionalism. We need to be able to evaluate our abilities and core competencies, to train and develop where necessary and beneficial, and to take responsibility for our own continuing professional development. This is in line with the codes of conduct and supervision principles we will cover in this chapter.

WHAT ATTRACTS US TO BECOME COACHES?

Coaches come from many backgrounds and follow their coaching career path in many different ways. There are coaches who have been in senior managerial positions for many years, and take on a coaching role within their organization. Some of those managers may choose to 'go solo' and start up a consultancy coaching business offering support that covers the spectrum from coaching through mentoring to training. They come from a corporate background with a wealth of experience. Other coaches go down the coach training route, deciding to make a career change and train to do so. They may also have managerial experience, but more commonly they are looking for a change in direction, believe they have the qualities to be a great coach, and support this with training and development.

If we only use our experience or only our training as coaches, we're missing a trick, and open ourselves up to potentially dangerous practice. If we remember Kate in Chapter 3, she reverted to her old management style and brought that into her coaching session. Her lower levels of regard for others impacted on how she operated as a coach/manager. And her negative attitude towards the benefit that the training could achieve got in the way of her being able to listen and coach effectively.

Most people come to coaching because they believe they can help others, and helping others fulfils their values. We need to be sure we're becoming coaches with a high self-regard. The danger is that occasionally someone wants to become a coach when he or she has a conditional self-regard of 'I am ok as long as I help others' running unconsciously in the background.

Anyone who lives his or her values on a daily basis is going to be authentic and fulfilled. The key to EI coaching is making sure that we're authentic *and* emotionally intelligent in our relationships with our coachees. This means acknowledging that they have their own values, which may or may not coincide with ours. We need to be aware of the impact we have in the coaching relationship. We also need to believe in our abilities as coaches and in the personal power our clients have to make changes that are right for them. We also need to provide something for our clients that demonstrates our intention to do all the above. A code of conduct is as important a document for our contracting purposes as professional indemnity insurance.

Supervision forms part of the coach's own development and best practice, and we hope our passion for the opportunities for reflection and further learning that supervision offers are apparent in this chapter.

SO, WHAT DOES BEST PRACTICE MEAN TO YOU?

Remember the KASH model from Chapter 1? This model also applies to delivering best practice; our way of being authentic as coaches and fulfilling the definition of coaching ethics as integrity in the moment of choice. We need the knowledge and skills of a coach *and* the attitudes and habits of highly effective, emotionally intelligent human beings. All four aspects of the KASH model have to be there for us to deliver best practice.

We asked 100 practising coaches what best practice means to them and here's a summary of their responses grouped into different aspects of what is required of a professional coach.

Coaching skills
- Delivering outstanding coaching.
- Broadening my coaching experience.
- Creating an environment conducive to outstanding thinking and development.
- Being trained to a high standard.

Reflective learning and development
- Keeping up to date with developments in the profession.
- Having supervision with a more experienced coach.
- Reflecting on my learning and skills.
- Having ongoing training in different aspects of coaching.
- Keeping a coaching learning journal.

- Engaging in learning experiences with other coaches – like action learning sets or coaching communities.
- Being coached myself.
- Operating with integrity.
- Monitoring and evaluating my coaching effectiveness.

Business practices

- Abiding by industry professional codes of conduct.
- Belonging to a professional body.
- Managing coaching/client relationships and projects to the highest level of accepted professional standards.
- Protecting client records and information.
- Demonstrating transparency of practice and informed consent.
- Keeping my client safe.
- Being professional: running my coaching business in a professional manner, treating my clients professionally.
- Maintaining confidentiality in alignment with the contract.
- Having clear and agreed contracts.
- Knowing my boundaries.
- Being safe.

Coaching as an emerging profession

- Keeping our minds open to the changes that may be affecting our profession and contributing to its evolution.

As one of the coaches said, 'Ethics guide the coach's behaviour and lifelong learning, both personally and in his or her business practice.'

What is your own definition of 'best practice' in the context of your professional role? What does it mean to you personally and professionally?

Activity: KASH analysis of best practice

You may be familiar with the idea of a SWOT analysis where you identify your Strengths, Weaknesses, Opportunities and Threats, and may well have done one already as part of your business plan. Here we use KASH as the analysis tool – what knowledge and skills do you have that help you deliver best practice? Which attitudes and habits support you in that? Fill in the quadrant in Figure 10.1.

There may be gaps you notice – take some time to reflect on what's there and working really well, and what could be improved.

Knowledge	Attitudes
Skills	Habits

Figure 10.1 The KASH quadrant

We saw in Chapter 2 that there are different definitions of coaching. The important thing is to be able to offer your services in an ethical, professional manner, and to be clear what you can and cannot achieve.

CRACKING THE CODE

As we work in an unregulated profession at the moment, there is no profession-wide consistent code of conduct. The established coaching bodies have their own, individual coaches have their own, training/coaching organizations have their own. It is important that we are transparent in what we do. We've already looked at the link between emotional intelligence and best practice; a code of conduct is simply something that we live by as authentic coaches, that we can give to our coachees to demonstrate our integrity and professionalism. Codes of conduct are essentially identified behaviours that demonstrate positive attitudes, robust values and healthy life positions.

An EI coach's code of conduct

Keeping EI at the front of our minds when creating our code of conduct will ensure we keep the code simple, focused and clear. You will find the EI coach code of conduct in the coaching toolkit in Chapter 9; here are the key elements.

Competence

Coaches must only work within their levels of competence:

- *Knowledge and skills:* we have been trained and are experienced, professionally qualified coaches.
- *Attitude:* we have high self-belief and high awareness of the limits of our competence.
- *Habits:* we demonstrate outstanding coaching and communication skills.

Continuing professional development

This is about reflective learning and competence development:

- *Knowledge and skills:* we attend relevant further training and develop higher level skills.
- *Attitude:* we learn from more experienced coaches and supervisors, which will enhance our performance.
- *Habits:* we have regular supervision, and monitoring and evaluation of the effectiveness of our coaching.

Boundary management and professional relationships

This concerns being aware of professional boundaries in our skill sets, competence and relationships. We need to know when to stop and how to manage the ending of a coaching relationship:

- *Knowledge and skills:* we know how to be assertive with clients and customers and we have wide and varied skill sets and the ability to manage difficult circumstances that might arise.
- *Attitude:* we have good self-belief, high awareness of ourselves and others and positive regard for coachees.

■ *Habits:* we display confident and assertive behaviour, and communicate clearly.

Confidentiality

We need clear terms and conditions of confidentiality, the circumstances under which it can be broken and how:

■ *Knowledge and skills:* we are aware of the circumstances under which confidentiality would be broken.
■ *Attitude:* we are non-judgemental and hold our coachees in high regard, whilst observing high self-regard.
■ *Habits:* we communicate clearly with our coachees.

Contracting

This is about establishing clear terms and conditions for the relationship before any coaching starts:

■ *Knowledge and skills:* we ensure we provide good, clear contracts.
■ *Attitude:* we respect our coachees, customers and ourselves.
■ *Habits:* we abide by the contract in all we do.

Respect for coaching as an emerging profession

Always acting in a way that does not bring coaching or mentoring into disrepute.

Keeping a high regard for ourselves and for those we work with, as well as for coaching as an emerging profession, will ensure our code is appropriate and relevant, without becoming pompous or overcomplicated. One of the primary coaching principles is that the coachee has the answers within him or herself, the coach's role is to help the coachee find them; the coaching relationship is based on the coachee's agenda, not that of the coach, and that the coach will not judge the coachee. This fundamentally supports the healthy life position of 'I'm ok, you're ok' and the emotionally intelligent coach will have the self-awareness to recognize when that life position might slip. By being aware of the impact of sitting in any of the other life positions as a coach, the practitioner is more likely to be able to deliver best practice with his or her client.

So how does a coach manage a situation where the client seems to present something that is outside of the coach's competence without appearing judgemental or critical? How does the coach stay within the healthy 'I'm ok, you're ok position'?

Adam's story

Adam was hired to coach Sam, a junior solicitor who was underperforming, regularly failing to meet deadlines and appearing to take several 'duvet days', contributing to poor attendance at work.

Sam's picture of himself was pretty low, and Adam helped him identify areas where he could start to build his self-esteem. Sam developed an action plan in conjunction with a reflective journal to note his progress.

In the third session Sam disclosed a specific incident earlier in his life that he believed was holding him back from being really successful as a solicitor. Adam felt out of his depth. Sam referred to the incident frequently through the session and at every turn felt that his past was coming back to haunt him. Adam knew he could not carry on working with Sam as his coach until the block had been removed, and didn't feel qualified or competent to continue.

He asked Sam how he'd found the coaching within the session, inviting him to be honest in his response. Sam reflected he'd felt frustrated and had become aware that he wanted to talk in much greater depth about the incident. Adam was able to share his thoughts that he didn't feel he was best placed to work with Sam in that context and asked Sam what solution he might have. Sam requested time to reflect and contact a counsellor. He thanked Adam for bringing up the topic for discussion.

What did Adam do well?

He was honest, picked up on his feelings and gave Sam the opportunity to come to his own conclusion about what to do next. Sam felt listened to, heard and respected, and more able to be open about what was going on for him.

When we look at the relationship management scales within the EI model, it is clear how our regard for others and our awareness of others impacts on the relationship the coach has with his or her client. The code of conduct elements of confidentiality, contracting and respect for the emerging profession sit well within these scales. When a coach or mentor has high regard for others, as well as high self-regard, then he or she is likely to see the relationship as an equal one. The EI coach will facilitate the client's own discovery and will be non-judgemental of the client's ideas, values and beliefs. The EI coach will keep his or her own values and beliefs out of the dialogue. The EI coach may pick up on coachees' moods more easily, sense when there's something else going on, and be able to use his or her intuitive coaching skills to excellent effect. If the coach is self-aware and also has good awareness of others, he or she will know how to keep his or her intuition real, will not make assumptions, and will give coachees the space and time to be able to explore their own way.

A little knowledge is a dangerous thing

Doug is a branch manager. He has a team of around eight working for him, and has been sent on a one-day coaching course by his area director. His director believes that Doug's management style could improve with better communication and interpersonal skills.

Doug enjoys the day course and returns to his branch full of enthusiasm with his new-found skills, looking forward to better levels of communication within the office. He brings his team together, hands out a 'Wheel of Team Effectiveness' that he used on the course and asks his team to complete it. He then asks them to share their feedback with the group. One of his team, Fiona, mentions a lower rating for 'management of other people', and Doug immediately comments that she shouldn't be doing the job she is if she can't manage people. Fiona is confused and upset by the comment, and is unwilling to share anything else within the session. She returns to her desk and says to her colleagues that this coaching is weird; it seems to knock people rather than empower them.

What happened here?

Doug's self-awareness and awareness of others seem to be low in this scenario. His enthusiasm for the skills he'd learnt in a short course had overtaken his ability to be aware of the impact his practice of those skills had on the team around him. His limited knowledge and lack of understanding about boundaries, best practice and ethics, combined with lower levels of awareness and even regard for others, led to a situation where his behaviour was totally inappropriate.

WHAT CONSTITUTES BEST PRACTICE FOR THE EMOTIONALLY INTELLIGENT COACH?

If we take the first four scales of EI (self-regard, regard for others, self-awareness and awareness of others) and link them with the best practice definitions above, we come at the whole aspect of ethics, codes of conduct and supervision from an holistic perspective. It's important to remember that our principles are based upon our values and beliefs, and therefore are individual. However, an ethical code of conduct needs to take account of more than just our individual values. It needs to have a wider perspective.

Let's look at the definition Allard de Jong gives us within the context of the emotionally intelligent coach: 'Coaching ethics: integrity in the moment of choice.' What has to happen for us to be able to show integrity in the moment of choice? We need to know what integrity means to us, and how we demonstrate that in our behaviour. We need to have good self-regard to believe that we can make the right choices in a heartbeat. We must be self-aware enough to recognize what's going on for us in that moment. We have to have sufficient awareness and regard for others to be aware of the impact of our behaviour or actions on our clients.

When you're coaching, how often do you get a sense that things are going well within the session? How do you know? What tells you that without anything being said by your client? You may pick up on the energy in your coachee's voice; on the motivation and decision making that's going on seemingly effortlessly. You may be aware of a sense of fulfilment. This is a sense that you're making a difference simply by asking questions that prompt outstanding thinking; that your silence is more powerful than any question you could ask. How do you know that? You may not be consciously aware of all of this in the session itself, but your unconscious brain is giving you the signals, you go with the flow and the session brings solutions from your client. What about when you get the sense that all is not well? Where do you feel that? How does it manifest itself?

In both these situations there is a double awareness happening. Awareness within yourself (you may even experience physical signs such as a hunching of your shoulders or dryness of mouth), and an awareness of what is happening for your coachee. Maybe he or she becomes more withdrawn if the session isn't going well, or displays passive or even aggressive behaviour. For us to deliver best practice and be ethical coaches, we need to activate that sense, our intuition if you like. Of course it is important that it does not distract from the session as there is no place for us focusing more on ourselves rather than the coachee. However, to be aware of what our body and brain tell us in the moment is also important. This enables us to show integrity in the moment of choice.

The coach's ok corral

For a coach to practise in an ethical way, his or her self-regard, regard for others, self-awareness and awareness of others must be high. Let's look at the implications of it being anything else. Here's a reminder of the life position grid and what the impact is of a coach sitting in any place other than 'I'm ok, you're ok'.

In Chapter 3 we looked at the impact of a coach being in each of the four quadrants when coaching, highlighting the importance of the coach staying in the 'I'm ok, you're ok' attitude set. Consider the impact on a coaching session or situation where the coach is demonstrating differing levels of self-regard and regard for others, as is the case in the following example.

I'm not ok You're ok Passive **The submissive coach:** subjective intentions about boosting coach's own self-regard	I'm ok You're ok Healthy Assertive **The EI coach:** successful, authentic, positive, objective intentions
I'm not ok You're not ok Stuck Passive-aggressive **The hopeless coach:** doubting success of coaching and possible benefits to client	I'm ok You're not ok Judgemental Aggressive **The directive coach:** subjective intentions about manipulating client

Figure 10.2   The coach's ok corral

Gill is coaching David, a team leader who is experiencing some challenges with one of his direct reports who seems to be taking frequent days off sick without really good reason. The situation reminds Gill of one of her employees in a previous career, whom she had to discipline because of similar behaviour.

The coaching session doesn't seem to flow, and Gill feels that David is being resistant to thinking more creatively about the challenge in front of him. She feels frustrated and is conscious that David is more withdrawn than in previous sessions. At the end of the session she asks him if he has achieved what he wanted to in the session. David tells Gill that he felt her questions were unusually forceful and that he felt rushed through the session.

Gill reflected on the coaching session later and acknowledged that she had felt quite frustrated with David as he didn't seem to be able to see that he needed to be more assertive. She recognized that she had linked his situation to her earlier one and had thought he needed to toughen up a bit.

Of course coaches are human and are emotional beings, so we will from time to time slip into a different quadrant. That's a fact. Being emotionally intelligent is *not* about being constantly in a bland 'nothing fazes me' state.

It is about being able to recognize what's going on for us, being able to acknowledge the emotion that's present and being able to respond and behave in a way that demonstrates high regard for both ourselves and those around us. An emotionally intelligent coach will use his or her high self-awareness to pick up on the fact that something has triggered a less than healthy response. He or she will reflect on ways to get back to the 'I'm ok, you're ok' quadrant if this happens.

HOW WAS IT FOR YOU?

Reflecting on our coaching skills and being able to acknowledge both the strong qualities and skills we have, as well as being aware of where there is room for development, shows strong emotional intelligence. Most coach training programmes encourage students to keep a learning journal, a log of their experiences as they develop their coaching skills. Many stop once they are coaching professionally, and yet a journal offers an opportunity to learn even more once we're coaching on a regular basis.

Imagine a concert pianist never listening to him or herself play. Imagine a stand-up comedian never writing new material. Imagine a pilot assuming the machinery and instruments are all working perfectly without checking it. It just wouldn't happen. They all continually look for ways to improve their skills and to check out different ways of being outstanding. Stephen Covey (19) talks about 'sharpening the saw' as his seventh habit of highly effective people. This is about developing the habit of self-renewal and interpreting the 'self' as having four parts – physical, mental, spiritual and social/emotional – all of which need regular nurturing.

Feedback is a great way of checking that we're doing the best we can do and it helps keep us on our toes. In Chapter 4 we looked at how we can measure the impact of coaching as far as determining the return on investment (ROI). By including some feedback mechanism within the coaching relationship we can build in some measurement of the human experience as well. We can ask for feedback from various quarters: our coachees, the organizations for whom we work, and ourselves. We can use a supervisor to offer observation on what he or she hears or notices, on what he or she picks up in our case studies or in the language we choose to use. We'll look at supervision a little closer later in this chapter, so for now will concentrate on feedback from our coachees and questions we can ask ourselves.

Many coaches have specific forms and documents they use with their coachees to create regularity in feedback. What worked well for you today? What could I have done differently that would have been even more helpful? What didn't work for you today? To create a way of regularly checking with ourselves, we can consider what we do presently to reflect on our coaching expertise. How do you know you are delivering your best in the coaching relationship?

Activity: Reflective learning

There are a number of questions we can ask ourselves: what worked well? What could I have done better? What will I do differently next time?

You could also ask yourself some emotionally intelligent reflective questions as well: what was my position in the ok corral in that session? Did I wander far from 'I'm ok, you're ok'? If so, what was going on for me? Was I distracted? Did the conversation remind me of anything?

What was I aware of during the session? What did my intuition tell me? What did I do with it? What feelings? What thoughts?

Did I display integrity in the moment of choice? How do I know that?

Did I have any blind spots where I missed something? How do I find out?

Within the organizational context, where you may be coaching as a line manager or as an internal coach, other questions may be helpful to reflect on your best practice. How does what I've heard today impact on my working relationship with this person? How does my working relationship with this person impact on my ability to coach non-judgementally and objectively?

Looking again at the four key scales within EI (self-awareness, awareness of others, self-regard and regard for others), it is beneficial to base questions around them, and reflect on our coaching practice from this perspective. If we do this we will be creating the opportunity to develop our emotional intelligence alongside our coaching expertise.

Self-efficacy and the EI coach

Self-efficacy is the belief in our own abilities to perform at our best. In terms of the ethical EI coach, this supports high self-regard and a positive life position of 'I'm ok, you're ok'. Developing good self-efficacy supports the EI principles, and high levels of emotional intelligence will underpin a coach's self-efficacy. Reflective learning and supervision go hand-in-hand with the development of a coach's positive self-regard and belief in his or her own abilities. Receiving constructive feedback from coachees as well as supervisors and peers in an emotionally intelligent environment will also contribute to increased self-efficacy. Is this not the real purpose behind a code of conduct and ethics: a way to become an authentic coach?

SUPERVISION – THE HELICOPTER VIEW

The great thing about being in a helicopter is the uninterrupted view, as the cockpit is pretty much entirely glass and has tremendous visibility. Often the co-pilot will be able to see something the pilot may have missed. They are able to talk to each other to make sure everything's clear and ask how things look from each of their perspectives. They will also have radio contact with someone on the ground to get better directions or instructions and they can move speedily to different perspectives to make sure nothing is missed. Being able to take a helicopter view of our coaching practices gives us a great all-round picture, seeing the coaching from different perspectives.

Supervision is so much more than having someone more experienced asking challenging questions about your clients, business and professional development. It offers the coach the opportunity to put a spotlight on his or her wellbeing, and it is in this light that EI has such a large part to play in the supervision relationship. Supervision challenges the coach to develop self-awareness and self-regard and it builds on the scales of emotional intelligence and looks at the impact of all of them on the coach in his or her professional and personal lives.

The Chartered Institute of Personnel and Development's definition of supervision is:

> a structured formal process for coaches, with the help of a coaching super-visor, to attend to improving the quality of their coaching, grow their coaching capacity and support themselves and their practice. Supervision should also be a source of organizational learning. (CIPD, 2006)

Michael Carroll, in *Integrative Approaches to Supervision* (2001) looks at a definition of both supervision and supervisors:

> Supervisors live the supervisory life; they don't just do something to others. The values of supervision are the values of life, the position and stance taken, the belief system underlying behaviour. Supervisors supervise themselves first of all before being supervisors to and of others.

In the same way as we are instructed, on a plane, to put an oxygen mask on ourselves first in the case of emergency before we help others, as professionals we need to help ourselves if we are to be competent and ready to help others. Many organizations now require that their executive coaches have an experienced coach to whom they can refer for ethical support and advice, and for that they may choose someone internally or use an external coach supervisor. They see the benefit of their coaches being aware of how they coach, what the impact is on the coachee and coach, and when there might be times they need the input of a more experienced coach. It protects the coach, the coachee and the organization against poor quality coaching and dangerous practice.

It is worth looking briefly at various supervision models that have been borrowed from therapists to coaches in order to be able to put the EI model into perspective. Kadushin (1976) started the ball rolling by stating in his seminal work, *Supervision in Social Work,* that supervision needs to maintain at least three basic functions:

1. Educative: the development of the supervisee.
2. Managerial: quality control.
3. Supportive: ensuring the supervisee is able to process his or her experiences.

Proctor (Inskipp and Proctor, 1993) refers to the normative, formative and restorative aspects of supervision:

- *Normative:* the supervisor shares responsibility with the person being supervised for ensuring that the supervisee's work is professional and ethical, operating within whatever codes, laws and organizational norms apply.
- *Formative:* the supervisor gives feedback to help the supervisee develop the skills, theoretical knowledge, personal attributes and so on to increase the supervisee's competence as a practitioner.
- *Restorative:* the supervisor is there to listen, support and confront the supervisee when the inevitable personal issues, doubts and insecurities arise.

In 1995 Peter Hawkins and Robin Shohet devised a 'Seven-eyed model' supervision model that is widely acknowledged and practised. It was first used within the counselling and psychotherapy profession, yet it offers a framework that suits coaches and mentors equally well. In the supervisory relationship, the supervisor makes a choice as to where he or she focuses attention, and at any one time in the supervision session there are at least four elements involved:

1. the supervisor;
2. the coach/mentor;
3. the client; and
4. the work context.

Looking at the various aspects of the coach's work from seven perspectives leads to the model's title. It is not our intention to describe in great detail the process of supervision. Several excellent reference books address this much more thoroughly, and we list them in the references at the end of this chapter. We simply want to show how, as an ethical and professional coach, you can work with and develop your own emotional intelligence through reflective learning, acceptance of help, and support from experienced peers. Through the supervision process you're also likely to develop a deeper understanding of the impact you have on the coachee, the relationship and yourself.

In a supervision session, the supervisor will make observations about how you coach and behave, and what the supervisor thinks and feels being with you. It is not the role of supervisors to try to find meanings, make connections or understand. They simply observe what takes place and how they respond to that. The supervisor concentrates on what you did in the session you're talking through, raising your awareness both of yourself and also your coachee's response. How did you engage feeling with thinking and doing? What did you pick up from your coachee and how did that impact on your feelings? How did you choose what questions to ask, which path to take?

Next, the focus of the supervisor is on the relationship between you and your coachee, and on the conscious and unconscious interaction between the two. Asking questions such as, 'If you were a fly on the wall, what might you have noticed?' encourages you to become aware of your interpersonal and intrapersonal intelligences being used during the session. Referring back to the ok corral life positions, the supervisor may ask you where you think you might sit while listening to your coachee. For you to be in any quadrant of the corral other than 'I'm ok, you're ok' is an unhealthy place to be, and you may need to challenge and explore what is going on in the relationship. Keeping this strong life position in mind when coaching will help keep you in the best place for your client.

Another thing the supervisor may encourage you to do is to examine what's going on for you in relation to your client. Does your coachee remind you of someone, and if so, do you then respond to the client as if he or she *were* that person? The key here for you as an emotionally intelligent coach is to be aware of what you are feeling, being able to engage your thinking brain and behave in a professional, non-judgemental way. Taking time at the end of each session to reflect on what's gone on within the session, not only during a supervision session, will help you develop your own EI as a coach.

Your supervisor may also ask you questions about and offer thoughts on how the relationship between you and the supervisor reflects and mirrors the relationship between you and your client. This should raise your awareness of the interaction between the various 'players' in the relationships. Effective supervisors also reflect on the impact of the supervision session on themselves and how they are responding to what they're hearing from you and to your coachee's situation. They then offer you their observations and thoughts, raising the opportunity to learn and explore even more about the relationships and how they are played out.

Finally, the supervisor asks questions about the bigger picture, such as how you maintain your wellbeing while coaching. How do you manage your business practice? How do you manage ethical and boundary management challenges within your business?

Supervision at its core is about self-management and relationship management. If we look at our interpretation of Howard Gardner's multiple intelligences of interpersonal and intrapersonal skills, we see how they support both self- and relationship management: *intrapersonal intelligence* – being intelligent in picking up what is going on inside us and doing what we need to do about it; *interpersonal intelligence* – being intelligent in picking up what is going on in other people and between other people and doing what we need to do about it.

Consider these questions:

- How can this be applied in a practical, emotionally intelligent sense to coaching practice?
- What happens when you find yourself responding to a coachee in a judgemental way?
- How do you keep an 'I'm ok, you're ok' position in a situation when you listen to a coachee who is displaying low self-esteem or negativity that seems immovable?
- How do you maintain a healthy state of wellbeing if the coaching context is draining to you, maybe reminding you of a similar situation you've experienced yourself?

We have explored codes of conduct and how professional coaches support their own development and wellbeing by abiding by ethical processes. We have also looked at how coaches can use the experienced coach supervisor to ensure best practice by exploring their own responses to their coachees, the coaching relationship and the feelings they're experiencing and how they deal with them.

If we take a look at Figure 10.3 we can see how the other scales of the EI model fit in with the inter- and intrapersonal intelligences of Gardner, and how they can support ethical best practice.

An integral part of the model is the reflective learning that is essential for the authentic development of the coach. Self-regard and self-awareness give us the opportunity to see our strengths and identify those areas that can be developed, and build reflective learning into our continuing professional and EI development process.

Coaches often encourage their coachees to start a journal at the outset of the coaching relationship to reflect on their learning, on their raised

Figure 10.3 How intrapersonal and interpersonal intelligence are connected to emotional intelligence

awareness, and to note any changes in their attitudes and behaviour. If we look at the benefits of that process, is it not absolutely relevant for the coach to continue the practice for themselves?

Let's now look at the inter- and intrapersonal intelligences of the model and at how the self-management scales contribute to our ability to be in the best place to coach. What's happening here, and how might the emotionally intelligent coach respond in this scenario?

Andrea

Andrea is working with a coachee whose particular challenge is similar to one that she experienced a couple of years previously, that of moving on after a broken relationship. Her coachee has worked through the emotional impact and is now looking to make some decisions about her career and new relationships.

Andrea received coaching herself through a similar period, and has made some positive, strong decisions that have served her well.

In the session Andrea becomes impatient as the coachee seems to be taking a while to make decisions. Her unconscious connection with her own previous experience comes through in the questions she asks and in the tone in her voice. Her client starts to close down in her responses, as the coach asks more closed, directed questions.

Let's take a look at what's happening, or rather not happening, in the scenario from the perspective of the less emotionally intelligent coach. Andrea probably has relatively good self-regard, having worked through a similar challenge and built her self-esteem again. However, her self-awareness, and indeed her awareness of others seem to be a little lacking. She is unaware of her own feelings and the way she's responding to them as well as not picking up on the feelings and withdrawal of her coachee.

The emotionally intelligent coach would have been able to pick up on the feelings of frustration earlier, engaged her thinking brain and realized that the coachee was becoming withdrawn and disengaged from the coaching process. In that moment she would have been able to be flexible in her approach, to refocus on the coachee and change the direction of her questions. By picking up on the tone of her coachee's responses and by being aware of what was happening in the session, she could have turned it around. She could have reflected back to the coachee at the end of the session what had happened, and taken responsibility for it.

By being emotionally resilient, the coach can address her own issues later, with a supervisor if necessary, and determine how she wants to handle the learning she's gained from her reflection.

Summary

■ From an ethical perspective, what has to be happening in order for us to be emotionally intelligent coaches engaged in best practice, working under a strong ethical code and reflecting on our learning to be the best we can be?
  - We have and abide by a strong code of conduct, one based on industry guidelines, preferably from a professional body whose code is accessible for all prospective coachees to see.
  - We conduct our businesses in line with that code, observing its elements of professionalism, continuing professional development and integrity. We ensure that our business practices reflect our authenticity.

- Ethical coaching means that we demonstrate integrity in the moment of choice.
- The EI coach's code of conduct is based on self-regard, regard for others, self-awareness and awareness of others.
- The key areas a code of conduct covers are competence, boundary management and contracting, continuing professional development, confidentiality and respect for coaching as an emerging profession.
- When we coach we should make sure we stay in the healthy 'I'm ok, you're ok' position, holding both our coachees and ourselves in high regard.
- It is important to think about why we became coaches, to make sure it's not about 'I'm ok as long as I'm helping others'.
- For the relationships with our clients and coachees to be mutually rewarding, we must be authentic and emotionally intelligent coaches, and encourage the same from our coachees.
- When reflecting on the quality of our coaching, it is important to review it using all aspects of the KASH model.
- Values, attitudes and behaviours form the basis of best practice for the EI coach.
- Reflective learning helps us develop as coaches and also to develop our own emotional intelligence.
- Supervision plays an ever increasing role in maintaining the provision of quality coaching.
- Coaching is about being authentic and the emotionally intelligent coach loves being authentic!

References

Carroll, M and Tholstrup, M (eds) (2001) *Integrative Approaches to Supervision,* Jessica Kingsley, London

CIPD (2006) *Coaching Supervision: Maximizing the potential of coaching,* Ref 3850, CIPD, London

Covey, S R (1999) *The 7 Habits of Highly Effective People,* Simon and Schuster, London

Gardner, H (1999) *Intelligence Reframed: Multiple intelligences for the 21st century,* Basic Books, New York

Hawkins, P and Shohet, R (2000) *Supervision in the Helping Professions,* Open University Press, Milton Keynes

Inskipp, F and Proctor, B (1993) *The Art, Craft and Tasks of Counselling Supervision. Part 2: Becoming a supervisor,* Cascade, Twickenham

Kadushin, A (1976) *Supervision in Social Work,* Columbia University Press, New York

Whitmore, J (2002) *Coaching for Performance,* Nicholas Brearley, London

Appendix 1

Interview with Sir John Whitmore

What is coaching?

There are probably a thousand different definitions of coaching, and how you define it somewhat depends on your perspective on the day. I'd like to give two examples:

One is to raise awareness and responsibility of the coachees, to assist them with their progress, productivity and performance.

Some people focus their definition on the coach's rules and behaviours. I don't believe in such a tight definition in that way. I would go the other way and say that coaching is being appropriate for the circumstance and the individuals in the moment, in order to facilitate them to move forwards in whatever way they want to.

Is coaching directive or non-directive?

It is a myth to say the coach is a vacuum and works entirely on the other person's agenda, because you as a coach alter the context merely by your presence with another human being. Whether we like it or not our presence has an influence and also the way we see the world ourselves determines the way we ask the questions that we ask. It is very important for us as coaches to set a broad context for our coachees to explore.

What is the difference between coaching and mentoring?

The mentor uses his or her knowledge and experience of the job, and say quite specifically, 'This is how it works here.' To be a mentor you need to be an experienced person in the field. To be a coach that experience can be a disadvantage as it could tempt you to steer or advise your coachees towards what you think is the solution rather than help them to find their own.

What impact can effective coaching have?

It's all about change, and hopefully change for the better. It moves people forward and it's the responsibility part that energizes that. You can take in a lot of information and not change, but when you take responsibility for the awareness that you have acquired, that drives the change. Self-responsibility has a dynamic effect.

What does it take to be a great coach?

Being a great coach takes practice, with awareness – you could drive 100,000 miles a year and not get any better, if you don't do it with awareness. As a coach you could coach 100 people and not get any better too, unless you pay a lot of attention to what you're doing and how it is received. That should not be in a self-critical sense; it's about being aware of what you're saying, how the coachee is responding and about your own behaviour.

What role does coaching play for the individual, organization and society?

Organizations are made up of individuals, and organizations exist in a society. A responsible organization will consider its impact on society – coaches with a broad vision will facilitate the relationships between individuals, teams, organizations and society. It is all a whole system.

(Sir John is involved in three particular areas right now, one being the use of coaching in prisons to assist rehabilitation, another has to do with cross-cultural conflict internationally, and the third is a European Commission project to change driver education from instruction to coaching. This is because coaching addresses self-responsibility and other attitudinal issues that are a huge, and all too often fatal, problem today with young male drivers.)

When does coaching not work?

Coaching does not work when the building's on fire. You don't ask your coachees what they smell; you get them out first, and then maybe ask, 'How could we have done that better?'

In a crisis people tend to do things themselves rather than tell others what to do because it is quicker. In an emergency I'm going to say to someone like an accountant, give me those figures now, not explain why. Normal management style should be based on principles of coaching. – 'How are you going to do this, and what resources do you need?'

What is the role of values, attitudes and beliefs in coaching?

Values, attitudes and beliefs have a big impact on the coaching process. Coaches' values will determine the type of questions they ask. Their own beliefs will determine the kinds of questions they ask as will their attitudes and assumptions. A big weakness in humankind is that we believe we know the truth; in fact we only operate on assumptions, not truths. There is a difference in 'truths' in different cultures. We live by the story that we create, and that determines how we operate. It is only our story and another person has a different story. The story that a coach has needs to be pretty sophisticated, and he or she needs to be broad and deep in consciousness. This is enormously important and far too little attention is paid to it in coach training.

If there were one secret to great coaching, what would it be?

Expand our own consciousness – many coaches and individuals feel they have to do another training, etc to increase their knowledge, but it's the inner work we need to do, and that can be much cheaper! Our society is too focused on externalities (to acquire an MBA or another IT skill); that's all quantitative stuff, but what we lack is the qualitative, ie the wisdom to use our knowledge responsibly, rather than just more knowledge.

What is the connection between EI and coaching?

It is the starting point of coaching. If you're emotionally intelligent, you'll tend to behave in a coaching way anyhow, even if you have never heard of coaching. When I'm training people to become coaches, I start with EI – it is the foundation stone. The first step to EI is self-awareness – that's where it begins; it reflects the core coaching principle of awareness.

What is the future of coaching?

The future of coaching is unlimited. Coaching is inextricably connected with leadership. What we are seeing globally is a crumbling of authority and the respect in which authority has been held. When you think of great leaders, you think about Ghandi, Lincoln, Nelson Mandela, etc. It's pretty hard to find one today. There is a high degree of cynicism about the quality of leaders today. That's largely because they are not able to cope with the speed of change, and they are short-sighted and so personally limited or immature. They should be pursuing the path of inner development rather than grabbing for external technical quick-fixes.

Appendix 2

Interview with Dr Patrick Williams

What is coaching (and what isn't it)?

Coaching is a unique relationship where a special conversation takes place about you. It's a unique way to relate to people conversationally that brings out their best, a way of empowering them to say what they've not said, dream what they've not dreamed, get what they've not got. You do use direct communication (which is different from directive communication). For example, 'I hear you want to write that book, but I'm not convinced by your energy – what's that about?' If I was being directive, I'd say, 'If you want to write a book you'll have to discipline yourself to write three hours per day, etc.'

What is the difference between coaching and mentoring?

Mentoring is working with someone where you are modelling how to do what you do. So for a high-level manager, it's about sharing the ins and outs of becoming that position. A coaching mentor can use coaching skills and offer possibilities to the client: 'This is how I do it', not, 'This is how you should do it.'

What impact can/does effective coaching have?

In the biggest sense it can be transformational, usually in the long term, but it can also be short-term. It is an opportunity for coachees to say and think things out loud they've probably not said to anyone objective. It opens up vistas and practical steps to get them there.

What does it take to be a great coach?

It takes a passion for serving the client. A great coach needs to believe that he or she is whole, capable and resourceful. I think coaches need to be well developed interpersonally and transpersonally. Humility, credibility, strong ethics and integrity are also important.

When does coaching not work?

When it's forced. The readiness level of the client has to be right; it won't work if a person is psychologically or emotionally stuck, not able to move forwards.

What's the secret ingredient for great coaching?

It's having 'coaching presence'. We as coaches need to prepare either in person or on the phone so we're sending our heart energy to the client, getting the distractions out of the way, which leads to authenticity. The brilliance of coaching comes when I'm present and remain curious, and comfortable with not knowing.

In what way do organizations misuse coaching?

Some organizations use it to 'fix' people or teach them, and sometimes people are 'sent' to coaches to turn their work profile around; this is remedial coaching.

What role do attitudes have within coaching?

They're important and apply both to the coach and the client. The attitude of the coach needs to be that the client is whole and resourceful.

Any negative attitude will affect the coaching relationship. Coaching itself can help shift clients' limiting beliefs/attitudes. Coaching is about thinking outside the box and identifying what you really want.

What is the link between coaching and performance?

Coaching in its best sense should unlock the potential and their performance will improve if the clients want to (there is the possibility they could find they're in the wrong pool!). Coaching empowers the person to be more self-responsible and responsive.

What role does EI have to play?

As a psychologist, when I came across EI, I thought, 'Finally you can talk about feelings'; there's a science to it, which is key and I am thrilled it came in the marketplace, a way to improve and measure how I am. Organizations with a command and control attitude of 'leave your emotions at home' lose out. Working with whole people you have to take emotions into account. EI is the missing link. It's what makes it sustainable.

What does the future of coaching look like?

It's big! The day may come where coaching supplants psychotherapy, certainly in the United States. It has been estimated that approximately 10 to 15 per cent of the population benefit from counselling. I believe most of the population could benefit from coaching. A coach approach could supplant the generally ineffective ways people communicate superficially so frequently.

The role of ICF will continue to be strong and will grow as a global organization and there will be other groups who meet the needs of coaches too.

Appendix 3

Interview with Tim Gallwey

How would you define coaching?

It's about evoking the best from people, including yourself.

What impact, in your experience, does great coaching have?

It increases performance, learning and enjoyment. It makes the person feel more in touch with his or her own competence to perform, learn and enjoy.

When does coaching not work?

When the coach doesn't really care. When the coach takes over the burden of the problem or the issue. When there is a judgemental atmosphere. When the coachee doesn't want to be coached. When the coachee feels too much self-doubt, inadequacy, or fear of failure or judgement.

What does it take to be a great coach?

A person who is willing to be themselves while staying within the limits of the coaching conversation – who can make the coachee feel safe (free of fear of judgement) while at the same time challenged to rise to the occasion. A person who can listen to the different levels of communication, who can stay clear about the goal, who can trust the inherent competencies in the person being coached. Integrity. Care. Passion for excellence. A willingness to not look for credit from solutions or progress.

What role can coaching play for individuals, organizations and society?

It can increase levels of performance, increase the rate and breadth of learning, especially from experience (largely through reflection), increase in self-motivation and enjoyment.

How would you go about measuring the impact of coaching?

Measure short- and longer-term levels of performance. The internal changes, which is what coaching affects, cannot yet be measured well.

What's the connection, in your opinion, between coaching and performance?

Coaching should have the impact of improved performance.

What role do values and attitudes have within coaching?

The attitudes and the values of the coach in relation to the coachee play a tremendous role in the effectiveness of coaching. They will either put the coachee in a receptive state of mind for learning and performance or not.

The attitudes and values of the coachee are even more relevant and are critical to the success of the coaching conversation.

What role does EI have to play?

The coach's empathy and understanding of that which interferes with performance and learning is critical to success. The client's emotional intelligence regarding his or her own interferences and own inner resources make a great difference in the ability to perform and to evolve in skill and understanding.

How do you see the future of coaching?

My hope is that it can facilitate the evolution of mankind at every level of human endeavour. My concern is that it will become dominated by concepts that leave out the intuitive understanding and enjoyment of coach and coachee. That it will become too systematic. That it will not exercise enough self-restraint in crossing lines into therapy or spiritual teaching.

Appendix 4

Interview with Kirsten M Poulsen, EMCC

Kirsten M Poulsen is Vice President of EMCC as well as President of EMCC Denmark. She states: 'In this interview I am expressing my personal views as well as some general views of EMCC on coaching and mentoring. Please be aware that in an inclusive organization, as EMCC is, there will be divergent views on the definition of coaching and mentoring among our members – as well as among our elected personnel.'

How would you define coaching?

To define coaching is a challenge. As an association we have a wide definition of coaching and do not distinguish between coaching and mentoring.

Creating development and facilitating learning on the conditions of the individual. The main point is about developing people within an ethical framework and ensuring quality.

EMCC has developed a competency framework to emphasize the need for quality in coaching – and this framework is the foundation for the EQA – EMCC's Quality Award which is given to coaching and mentoring education programmes (see website: www.emccouncil.org).

The core skills of the competency framework are about knowing yourself, understanding the process and having the right techniques to do this, and also thinking about the ethical dilemmas you may face in coaching.

What impact can effective coaching have?

I would describe it as an accelerated learning process, in the sense that without coaching it would take you longer to reach the same insight and learning, especially if you are talking about coaching being about setting and achieving goals.

What role does coaching play for individuals, organizations and society?

An important role but we should be aware that coaching cannot solve everything. The coaching style is a very good way of handling people, employees and managers in the knowledge society. I think the reason why coaching and mentoring are very hot and popular is because we exist today in a very individualistic society. Everybody is very focused on self-realization and really using all their talents. This requires managers to be more aware of the individuals and to behave as a leader rather than as a manager. You have to work with staff in a different way and I think coaching is a great tool for that, for showing peers/employees you really care about them as people and not just as tools or as cogs in a big machine. In that sense, both coaching and mentoring are key tools for attracting and keeping good people, but they are not the only tools.

When does it not work?

When managers hire you to 'fix' their employees – that is a no-go! Also, if the person doesn't have knowledge, coaching won't work – coaching is about creating new insights and learning, and you cannot achieve new factual knowledge that way.

If there were one secret ingredient to coaching, what would you say it would be?

It's the miracle of the moment and you never know when it's there.

How is coaching misused by organizations?

Fixing people. Thinking this is a miracle tool. Some companies use it as a way to buy absolution for when things aren't working.

What is the link between coaching and performance?

It depends on what type of coaching we're talking about. The main idea of coaching is creating learning even before performance. When you gain new insights and new learning, you should be able to perform better. The key is coaching – learning – performance.

What do you feel is the link between EI and coaching?

EI is about knowing yourself, knowing what you're good at and what you're not good at and being very aware of yourself in the coaching conversation. In that sense, EI is a way to gain better awareness and become a better coach. In my own company we have done some research that shows that mentors need at least the same or a higher level of emotional intelligence than their mentees – it does have an effect on the mentoring relationship.

What does the future of coaching look like?

I would hope major organizations in the field, such as EMCC and ICF, find a way of really communicating to the market the quality standards and the criteria to look for when selecting coaching and mentoring and that coaches and consultants will follow these guidelines on quality and ethics.

EMCC really connects the buyers, the coaches, the researchers and we share the experiences through our annual conferences. It's really important to help us all become better and focus on excellence and quality. I would love to see more of that.

In Denmark, the law now allows for companies to offer individual coaching as an employee benefit that can be deducted on company expenses even though it's for the individual only (like health insurance, or free lunches) – this can be good or bad – because in some ways you shouldn't see coaching as a commodity. On the other hand, it is also becoming more recognized and it will be interesting to see what effect it will have on the market. Coaching in Denmark is growing and booming as it is in Norway and Sweden.

Will the industry become regulated?

EMCC and ICF are doing some lobbying together. I'm not sure if regulation will come in. It would be nice if we could do it voluntarily as professional bodies.

As an association we want to see coaching making a difference and the right quality of coaching and mentoring is important. Our vision is that whoever uses coaching and mentoring does it in the right way and then it will have an impact.

Index

6/09